Laura

ROADS IN

A Ghost Hunter's Journey Continues

Stay Spooky!

Greg Feketik

gefeketik@gmail.com
www.gefeketik.wixsite.com/author
www.tcghohio.org

Edited by Shannon Dillon

Printed by CreateSpace, an Amazon.com
Company

I would like to thank everyone who encouraged me to finish my second book. You know who you are.

I would also like to thank my sister Shelley Grant and her husband Jim for always making our little trips together fun and interesting.

Thank you to everyone who gave me permission to use photographs in this book: Summit Metro Park system, Lemp Mansion, Sharyn Luedke, owner of the McPike Mansion, the Ruebel Hotel, Historic Royal Palaces, Janice McBride McCreadie, Rosslyn Chapel Trust, Edinburgh City Council Parks, Green Space and Cemeteries, Day of the Dead Tours, Dalhousie Castle, the Myrtles Plantation, the Roads Hotel and South Shore Community Development Corporation.

Thank you to Bill Przybylowicz and Harold Avalos for sharing your stories with me about St. Joseph Hospital.

Special thanks to Jim Janasko for allowing us, over the past two-and-a-half years, to help make St. Joseph Hospital into something good for the community. It's too bad it had to end, but it was fun and worthwhile while it lasted.

Special thanks to Janice McBride McCreadie and her husband Alec McCreadie for making our trip to Scotland fun and memorable.

This book is dedicated to my parents George and Arlene. I hope you're proud of me. I think of you every day...love and miss you.

Extra special thanks to my wife Kathy who puts up with me every day of the year. She is also my favorite co-investigator and a driving force in my life. I love you!

TABLE OF CONTENTS

Chapter One

<u>BELIEFS</u>

Why do some people believe in ghosts and others do not? What makes ghosts seem so normal and real to perfectly sane people from all walks of life and utter nonsense to others? Let us look at some statistics on people's beliefs reported in the December 2013 Harris Interactive Poll[1]. The poll revealed that 42% of Americans believe in ghosts. I was actually surprised to see almost half of the population believes in ghosts.

Here are some other interesting statistics from that poll.

Americans who believe in:
God – 74%
Heaven – 68%
Survival of the soul after death – 64%
The devil and hell – 58%
Theory of Evolution – 47%
Ghosts – 42%
Creationism - 36%
UFOs – 36%
Astrology – 29%
Witches – 26%
Reincarnation – 24%

I'm sure no matter which poll you look at, the numbers will be somewhat comparable.

There are several interesting and somewhat contradictory beliefs I noticed about this poll. The first thing I found amusing is the belief or should I say the non-belief in witches. Only 26% of people polled believe in the existence of witches, when in fact witches are real. I'm not talking about the broom-riding, green-skinned, wart-on-the-nose, pointy-hat type of witch from movies and television, but modern witches. In today's society there are thousands, if not millions of women and men who practice the art of witchcraft. There are numerous types of witches, from Green Witches who focus on natural places and things through Mother Nature, to Black Witches who perform acts, which are spiteful and harmful to others. I think the main argument here is not if there are witches, but are witches, through the art of witchcraft, able to cast spells, both for good and evil purposes? The practical side of me says it is impossible for them to cast spells on people, but the other side of me, which believes anything can be possible, to a certain degree, thinks why not? A lot of people believe in healing powers and miracles and pray for help when things are not going well for them, family members or friends. I see it numerous times on social media sites, where someone asks others to pray for their sick grandmother, father, sister, etc. So why not believe witches can cast spells? I have even had others pray for me when I became sick.

In March 2015, I had a total knee replacement on my left knee. I already had four surgeries on that knee, the first one occurring in 1977 when I was only 19 years old. After almost 40 years of knee problems and pain, it was now time to get the troublesome knee replaced. After I had the surgery, I started to have complications from the medication I was on, which was making me constipated. The surgery was actually easier than what I was going through now! I was worried that I would eventually have some sort of blockage in my intestines. Not to get too graphic, but I tried everything, including stool softeners, prune juice and whatever else I thought might work. After some painful days, everything started returning to normal. Then on April 1st, I had the worst pain I have ever had in my life in my lower left abdomen. I was doubled over in agony. My son's girlfriend, who was staying with us at the time, became worried because she didn't know what to do to help. At that moment, I didn't think anything would have helped. I called my wife Kathy at work and told her I was in extreme pain and didn't know what to do. She immediately left work and drove home, where she found me on the sofa, white as a ghost and in extreme pain. She told me we needed to go to the emergency room ASAP and like any typical guy, I told her no. I figured it was probably just gas - the worst gas I ever had. Needless to say, I lost the argument and Kathy took me to the emergency room. Once at the ER, I was given morphine to help with the pain, but it didn't help much. The ER doctor requested several tests, including a blood test and a CAT scan of my abdomen. The results of the CAT scan came up inconclusive, and a blood test showed an elevated white cell count. The doctor suspected there was something going on that she wasn't able to diagnose at the emergency room and admitted me to the hospital. I was transferred by ambulance to the hospital for further testing. In the meantime, Kathy contacted a family friend and told him to contact Cat Young and Tess Hughes, who live in Tennessee. Cat and Tess are a mother and daughter team who are spiritual healers, known as the Mountain Gypsies. Kathy told the family friend nothing about what I was experiencing, only that I was really sick and needed some immediate healing.

Kathy arrived at the hospital a short time later. When she entered my room and saw me laying in the bed, she thought I was dying. I thought I was dying! When she asked how I felt, I replied in a weak voice, "I don't think I'm going to make it." My color was ashen, I was cold and clammy to the touch, and my breathing was shallow and labored, like I was heading toward my last breath. I was so weak I could barely talk.

I was still in extreme pain and the morphine was not helping at all. Eventually another CAT scan was done, but this time with contrast. Once again, the results were inconclusive. The doctors were baffled and could not figure out what was wrong. They suspected a blood clot, but no blood clot was showing up on the CAT scans. They decided to give me Heparin injections just in case there was a blood clot that was missed.

Cat and Tess were updated and told I was in the hospital and needed some healing prayers sent my way. I found out later that Tess woke up that same morning with an intense pain on the left side of her abdomen, in the exact same place my pain was located. Tess told her mom about the pain and they suspected someone, somewhere was going through the same thing. When Cat was contacted she said she saw a large blood clot on my left side. Remember, she had no clue as to what I was experiencing, only that I was sick and in the hospital. Cat relayed that the doctors were confused and they needed to work fast. Cat said she and Tess would be "praying" and "working" on me throughout the evening.

Later that evening, I actually started to feel better. The pain was finally subsiding, my color was returning to normal and I was regaining my strength. It was like one second, I was on my deathbed, the next I was wondering why I was in the hospital. The doctors were stumped and could find no reason for the quick turnaround.

They wanted me to spend the night for observation and more tests, but I decided I didn't need it, because I had spiritual help and felt 100% better!

After I was released from the hospital, I contacted Cat and Tess to thank them. They stated they prayed for me until the early morning hours. "Wow," I thought! I was amazed and in awe. Was it their prayers that healed me? I thanked them for everything they did, but they told me it wasn't them. They said they work through God and he is the one who healed me. I couldn't understand how that all worked. I was mystified, but I do have to admit I improved quickly and was very thankful of that!

Now, Cat and Tess are not witches; they call themselves gypsies, but do you think "witches" could accomplish the same thing or some other "miracle" or deed, good or bad, by praying to whatever god or entity they believe in?

The other thing I noticed about the poll was the questions on religion. I don't want to get into an in-depth discussion about religion - that's not what this book is about, but I think it's important to discuss some of it to a point. When you look at the religion aspect of the poll listed previously, the numbers just don't make sense…at least to me. How can 74% of Americans believe in God, yet only 68% believe in Heaven and 58% believe in the devil and Hell? Many people believe that it is written in the Bible (Ezekiel 28:12-19 and Isaiah 14:12-14[2]) that Lucifer, also known as Satan and the devil, among other monikers, was cast out of Heaven along with one-third of all the angels to rule in the pits of Hell.

How does one choose what aspects of the Bible and religion to believe in? Miracles, Heaven, Hell, Satan, spirits and the soul are all written in the Bible, yet the number of people who believe in those is less than the number of people who believe in a Christian God.

Every religion has their God(s) and most of them have God's adversary – good vs. evil. Buddhism has Māra, Islam has the Shaitan or Iblis (Iblees), and Judaism and Christianity have Satan.

So why are the numbers so off? To me it is contradictory to what people say they believe in and what they do not.

The answer is simple. People have free will to choose whatever they wish to believe, be it on faith, personal experiences or just going with the crowd. There are scientists who need scientific proof that something exists who believe in God. There are Atheists who believe in ghosts and the paranormal. It is all confusing and a lot of people's beliefs and non-beliefs confuse the hell out of me -- or am I putting too much thought into it?

Take me for example. I am not the most religious person in the world by any means and if I had to classify myself, I would have to say I'm an Agnostic. For me, I need to have some sort of proof, evidence or logical hypothesis that something exists or could exist. As far as my religious views (I was raised Catholic), there is no substantial proof or evidence that there is a God or Satan for that matter. A lot of you will disagree with me. It is all a matter of faith, which reminds me of a scene from the 1985 vampire-horror movie, *Fright Night*[3], starring Chris Sarandon as the vampire, *Jerry Dandridge*. One particular scene has the great vampire hunter, *Peter Vincent*, played by Roddy McDowell, confronting the evil vampire, brandishing a crucifix and saying, "Back, spawn of Satan!" Dandridge replies, "Oh, really?" grabs the cross, crushes it in his hands and throws it aside, saying, "You have to have faith for this to work on me!"

Let's talk about another subject that also creates a great deal of controversy -- aliens and UFOs. According to the poll, only 36% of Americans believe in UFOs and life on other planets. This is less than the amount of people who believe in ghosts, which really surprises me. Is it possible that we are the *only* intelligent beings alive in this vast universe, living on this tiny piece of space rock we call Earth? When I say vast, I do mean VAST! Genesis 1:27[4] simply states, depending on what Bible version, "So God created man in his own image…" Does that mean we are truly the only living things that were created in His image in this whole universe? That just doesn't make sense to me. Why would He create this vast universe and only create humans on this tiny speck of dust drifting through space? Again, we are talking faith, and to me it is not logical that we are the only ones living in this vast universe.

Try this one night when the night sky is clear and the stars are shining brightly. Lie under the stars and look up. Now imagine that one of those tiny stars you're looking at is a galaxy ten times larger than our own Milky Way galaxy, the galaxy in which Earth is located. Now just imagine in that one galaxy there are hundreds, if not thousands, of planets. Now imagine if just 1% of those planets was Earth-like and could possibly support life -- intelligent life. That means in that one small star you looked at, there could be as few as ten planets that could possibly harbor life. Now go to the next star, and the next star and the next. You know where I'm going. Just from the stars you can see where you are standing, there could be thousands, if not hundreds of thousands of planets that could have the right conditions to support life, and possibly intelligent life. But that's just from your view. Remember when you're looking at the night sky, that the Earth is round and no matter where you are, United States, Brazil, Canada, Australia, Greenland, Argentina or even Antarctica, the stars will be different and the stars keep going and going and going in multiple directions. It seems unfathomable to me that our universe keeps going and going, but it does, and if not, where does it end and what is on the other side? My brain really starts to hurt whenever I think about it, because I cannot comprehend how vast the universe really is! In fact, recent scientific estimates put the number of planets that could possibly support life around 500 million planets, and that is just in our own Milky Way galaxy![5] Inconceivable! Saying there is no intelligent life out there somewhere is like 15th century Europeans saying the Earth is flat and you'll fall off the edge if you sail too far west. Of course, they were wrong and soon discovered other people living in undiscovered lands such as the Native Americans, Mayans, Incas, Aztecs and others. Are we as narrow minded as our ancestors were and believe we are the *only* living things in the universe?

In Erich von Daniken's book, *"Chariots of the Gods? Unsolved Mysteries of the Past"*[6] written in 1968, he theorizes that the technologies and religions of many ancient civilizations were given to them by "ancient astronauts," who were welcomed as gods. In other words, aliens from other worlds visited this planet centuries ago. It is a very interesting theory to say the least and not many people agree with it, but let's just say from this vast universe there were aliens who visited this planet centuries ago. How would the people of the day react? We know ancient civilizations worshipped the stars, moon and sun and believed their gods lived up in the heavens, so it makes you wonder who or what they were worshiping.

I know I may sound contradictory in a few of my beliefs, but the things I believe in have "evidence" and witnesses. I definitely believe there could be intelligent life on other planets. There are too many eyewitness sightings, which sometimes include video and photographic evidence. There are also numerous witnesses and "evidence" (photographs, video and audio) captured during paranormal investigations.

Let us look at another highly controversial subject, Bigfoot, also known as Sasquatch. As far as Bigfoot goes, I do think there could be something like Gigantopithecus living in remote parts of California, Oregon, Washington and parts of Canada, commonly known as the Pacific Northwest. Here again, there are hundreds of eyewitness sightings, including some video and photographic evidence, along with physical evidence like footprints and hair. What are all of these witnesses seeing if it is not Bigfoot? The closest known animal that these witnesses could be seeing are bears, but are all of these reports a case of mistaken identification? I highly doubt it. Gigantopithecus[7] is an extinct genus of ape that existed as recently as 100,000 years ago. Fossil records indicate that Gigantopithecus was the largest ape that ever lived, standing almost 10 feet tall and weighing nearly 550 pounds, about the same size as reported Bigfoot sightings today.

There have been species of animals that were thought to be extinct, only to be discovered living. Take the Coelacanth[8] for example. This "extinct" fish, measuring almost seven feet long and weighing some 200 pounds, was thought to have died out 66 million years ago until a living specimen was caught in 1938 off the east coast of South Africa. Since that time, other Coelacanths have been caught and as of right now, scientists estimate their world population to be fewer than 500 animals -- not too bad for something that hasn't been seen alive for 66 million years.

Just because you've never seen an animal doesn't mean it doesn't exist or hasn't existed. I have never seen a dinosaur or sperm whale, but I know they are real animals that did or still exist. Thousands of new species of animals, insects and plants are being discovered every year, including new species of deer, monkeys, fish, cats, rodents and dolphins, just to name a few.

Creatures described as monsters in legend turned out to be real animals, such as the mountain gorilla discovered in 1902, the Komodo dragon discovered in 1910 and the giant squid discovered in 2004. What other unknown creatures are living in our unexplored jungles, forests, mountains, oceans and universe?

So why can't ghosts exist? As far as ghosts and spirits are concerned, you could probably call me a skeptic believer. There has been plenty of "evidence" gathered to seem to support the existence of ghosts and spirits -- everything from video recordings of unexplained phenomenon to unearthly voices captured on audio to thousands and thousands of personal experiences. The problem is the majority of the evidence collected has not been done so in a scientific manner and that's why mainstream science does not accept the existence of ghosts, just like they don't accept the existence of Bigfoot and other areas such as UFOs and the paranormal. Nothing exists until science proves that it exists.

I have plenty of "evidence" and personal experiences in my years of investigating, but to me, there still could be some logical or natural explanation that I haven't found yet. Because of all the evidence gathered, does it mean that ghosts are real? Obviously not. Do I believe in ghosts? Sure, to a point. I believe it's a possibility they may exist, but exactly what they are, I don't know and it is a fact that no one else knows either. Everyone has their own theories and beliefs as to what ghosts are and your guess is as good as anyone else's.

There are several theories and beliefs about what ghosts actually are: 1) A ghost is the soul of someone who has died and for whatever reason has not crossed over to the other side. They probably don't realize they're dead and stay in limbo until they find a way to cross over; 2) A ghost is an angel or a demon sent to protect or trick us; 3) A ghost is a being from an unknown dimension that can cross back and forth into our dimension -- a sort of time traveler; 4) A ghost is a residual imprint in the atmosphere at a particular location; 5) Ghosts are some sort of natural phenomenon that we cannot explain; 6) Ghosts are in our minds. We make them real because we want them to be real.

As stated earlier, it is all about your faith and beliefs. If you have a strong enough belief, no one will ever change your mind. A simple example of this in the paranormal field is the orb phenomenon. You know what I'm talking about -- those translucent balls of light with concentric circles captured in video and photographs. You see them constantly in photographs, books, television and on the internet. I don't want to burst anyone's bubble, but orbs are *not* paranormal in nature. Believe me! Ninety-nine-point nine percent of the time orbs are dust, bugs, rain, fog or moisture. Trust me on this, folks! A true orb can be seen with the naked eye emitting its own light. But it really doesn't matter what I say, I will never change the mind of the believers of orbs. We will be discussing orbs more closely later on in this book.

The bottom line is it really doesn't matter what your beliefs are because there are definitely things happening on this Earth and universe that cannot be explained.

Chapter Two

SIGNAL TREE

A NATIVE AMERICAN WARRIOR

Signal Tree, also known as Indian Signal Tree[9], is a mighty burr oak tree (photo 1) located in Akron, Ohio's Cascade Valley Park, part of the Summit Metro Park system. The majestic and massive tree stands over 100 feet tall and has an average spread of 75 feet. It is estimated that this tree sprouted sometime between 1675 and 1725. What also makes this interesting is the fact that burr oaks are rare in Northeast Ohio.

Photo 1 - Indian Signal Tree – Akron, Ohio

This park is one of the most haunted outdoor locations I have ever investigated and was one of our first investigations with a new local paranormal team that my wife Kathy and I joined in 2005. I was very hesitant when the founders of the group suggested we investigate this location. We had recently investigated an outdoor location several months earlier and nothing paranormal happened at all.

I personally don't enjoy investigating outdoor locations for several reasons. There are numerous natural sounds such as insects chirping, wind blowing through trees and bushes, planes flying overhead, and even cars and trains in the background that can make reviewing audio very difficult, if not impossible. When reviewing photographs and videos insects, pollen and other types of debris blowing around can be mistaken for paranormal activity. Besides, I didn't join a paranormal team to investigate places I could investigate on my own -- I have already done that. I wanted to investigate private businesses and homes to help people who are experiencing strange activity in their surroundings. I wanted to be able to make them feel comfortable in their home or workplace. How haunted could an outdoor location be, unless it was a cemetery? Even though there are some well-known haunted cemeteries in the United States, including St. Louis Cemetery #1 (New Orleans, LA), Resurrection Cemetery (Justice, IL), Cemetery Hill (Gettysburg, PA), Boot Hill (Tombstone, AZ), Hollywood Forever Cemetery (Los Angeles, CA) and Stull Cemetery (Douglas County, KS), I still have my doubts about cemeteries being haunted. Why would a cemetery be haunted? The deceased have no ties there except the shell of their previous flesh, bones and body. More than likely, there were no tragic events that would keep spirits lingering around a cemetery. Why do you think cemeteries may be haunted? This could be a great topic for discussion.

I had no prior knowledge of any paranormal activity reported at Signal Tree, but I decided to go and check it out. Who knows, maybe something will happen this time. First and foremost, what is Signal Tree and why is it called that? Signal Tree is an oak tree with not one main trunk, but three. Native Americans such as the Iroquois, Seneca, Ottawa, Delaware and Mingo used to make Northeast Ohio, and the Cuyahoga Valley in particular, their home. The Cuyahoga River runs through the valley and was a major resource to the local tribes for its water, fishing and transportation. Signal Tree is roughly 175 yards from the river and many believe the tree was manipulated as a sapling to form its trident trunks to be used as a "road" marker for the area tribes. The Indian Signal Tree marked the path for those traveling down the Cuyahoga River to the Portage Trail. The Native Americans would know from the signal tree that they could portage their canoes to Summit Lake which connected to the Tuscarawas River. By traveling on the Tuscarawas River, the Native Americans could travel all the way to the Ohio River. Hmmm. Native American grounds? I knew from past research that Native American grounds were held to be sacred and spiritual and could be extremely haunted. Could this be the case here? Was this sacred and spiritual ground? There was only one way to find out -- go on the investigation. So, that's what we did on a clear night in early November 2005.

Since this was a county park that closes at dusk, we obtained permission from the Summit Metro Park system for us to be there after hours. Remember to *always* obtain permission from the property owner or person authorized to give consent prior to investigating after hours or any time for that matter. It's not only polite, but you also don't want to risk the chance of being arrested for criminal trespassing. It is also an excellent idea to have written permission on your person just in case someone questions you.

By the time we arrived it was already dark. A Summit Metro Parks ranger met us as we arrived, stating he heard we were going to be there investigating and thought it would be interesting if he could stay and watch. We told him we had no problem with him staying, besides it was his park, and it was good having him there during the investigation, mainly for security and secondly, he could make an excellent witness if he observed anything out of the ordinary.

It was a very clear and peaceful night, with the outside temperature hovering around 52-55 degrees Fahrenheit. In fact, it was eerily quiet and still with no noticeable wind. It was almost too quiet, sort of like the calm before a storm. The moon was a waxing crescent with only 14% illumination, so it was a dark night with the stars peeking in and out of slow-moving clouds. It seemed like whatever was there was waiting for us, luring us into a state of false security before it sent its wrath down upon us. At least that's the feeling I had when I arrived. I wondered who or what types of creatures were watching us from the tree line? Were they living creatures or was it something else that used to walk these grounds a few hundred years ago? So, began our investigation at the haunted Signal Tree.

The investigators included three members of our paranormal team, along with my daughter Allison, my wife Kathy and myself. We walked around the tree and surrounding area, videotaping and taking photographs in the quiet darkness. We walked down a lonely footpath through the darkened woods and stopped to conduct an EVP (Electronic Voice Phenomenon) session. "Who is here with us? Why are you still here? Was this your land?" …no response. An EVP session is when an investigator asks questions of the ghosts or spirits in the hopes that a response, which is unheard at the time, will be captured on the audio and/or video recorder. Maybe they did not understand English. This was once Native American land, so maybe we needed to speak in their native language or maybe this place wasn't haunted after all. I kept telling myself the night was still young, but I didn't think we would capture any evidence, let alone have any personal experiences. Chances are nothing was going to happen and even if anything did, it could take hours. A few hours later into the investigation, Allison, who was taking photographs with a Canon PowerShot G6 7.1-megapixel digital camera, said she captured something strange in one of the photographs. The photograph in question showed a white, misty shape forming in front of the tree. You can see the tree directly behind the mist and to the right of the photograph (photo 2). The first 68 photographs were

all normal. "Well it's only one. Nothing to get too excited about. Let's see if we capture anything else," I said. I don't get too excited over one small piece of possible evidence -- it has to be something pretty spectacular to get me excited.

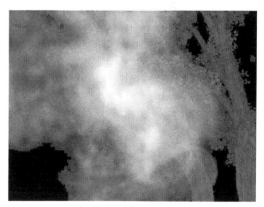

Photo 2 – Unusual mist

It was now getting late and nothing was really happening, so it was decided that four of the investigators would perform a séance near the tree. Kathy would participate, Allison would take photographs of the séance and I would videotape the seance. I was never into participating in the séances that this particular paranormal team conducted. Instead, I would monitor and document the session using EMF devices, temperature gauges, digital cameras and video cameras. I video recorded this séance, using a hand-held Sony HC-40 Mini-DV with

Night Shot. Hopefully, we would be able to capture any type of evidence on video.

The séance began with everyone standing near the inscription rock holding hands, at which time the rules of the séance were laid down to ensure everyone's safety during the séance. The inscription rock is a rock with a plaque near the tree that tells the history of Signal Tree. A primary concern during the séance is the safety of all involved, because if not properly conducted, negative and unwanted spirits may enter the circle. Some of the rules are to never release hands no matter what because this breaks the circle and also to never look behind you. If mirrors are present near the séance, they are always covered because it is said mirrors can be portals to the other side. Obviously, we did not have to worry about mirrors during this particular séance.

Our medium asked all involved to request protection from whatever religion or god they believe in to prevent anything evil or negative from entering the circle. All of the participants were then asked to imagine themselves enclosed in a bright, white light to protect them from all that is evil and negative. The medium continued, "As you start imagining yourself within that protective light, you can start feeling the energy flowing through your body into the person next to you." The participants then tried to communicate with any ghost or spirits that may be around and to let them know we come in peace and are not there to harm them in any way.

Several minutes into the séance, Kathy started to see a very vivid image of a Native American in her mind. She saw him so clearly that she could see the muscles and veins in his biceps bulging. He appeared to be some sort of great warrior and his face showed a fierceness that made her nervous. He appeared to be angry about something. Was he upset with the white man invading his land and home, or was he upset with us being there trying to communicate with him? Kathy was starting to feel more uneasy and nervous.

While Kathy was having her vision, I was video recording while standing on a dirt path near the séance (photo 3). Allison and the park ranger were sitting on a bench near where the séance was being held, watching to see if anything would happen. Allison continued to take photographs of the séance and the surrounding area. All of a sudden, I was pushed from behind by some unseen force! One minute I'm standing there minding my own business and the next, I felt a great pressure in the middle of my back driving me forward down the path! I was not walking, but sliding down the path! It was incredible! I couldn't believe what just happened! Somewhat in shock, I timidly said to the others, not knowing if they would believe me, "Something just like pushed me. Wow, that was weird. I felt this pressure on my back." Allison, who witnessed the whole incident,

Photo 3 – Author videotaping the seance

started laughing. When I asked her later why she laughed, she said it looked so funny and unnatural, "You were sliding down the path, but your feet weren't moving!" I also need to make everyone aware that the path was not sloping downhill in any way. It was very flat and level.

After the séance was over and the circle was closed, everyone asked me what had happened. I told them that something unseen had pushed me while I was videotaping the séance. Kathy then told us about the Native American she had envisioned during the séance, explaining how clearly, she had seen him and how menacing he looked. Kathy said she asked him if he was the one haunting this place could he push one of us to prove that he was here. It was precisely after she asked this question that I was pushed.

After the séance, we discovered strange anomalies in several of the photographs that Allison took during the séance.

Photo 4 shows a bluish-colored mist forming in the top left corner just above the group. The tree is located just to the left in the photograph.

Photo 4 - Anomaly in top left portion of photograph

Does it look like a face with two dark eye sockets surrounding the bridge of the nose starting to form? Or is it something else entering or coming out of the medium during the séance? What do you think?

Photo 5 shows what appears to be the profile of a face on the left side of the photograph. Could this be the spirit of the Native American Kathy had seen in her vision? Could it also be the spirit that pushed me? Again, the tree is located to the left in the photograph.

Photo 5 - Anomaly on left side of photograph

Photo 6 shows another bluish-colored mist materializing in the upper right portion of the photograph. If you look closely, you can see what appears to be the face of a bear or wolf forming. What seems to be two eyes and a snout are clearly seen. Bears and wolves are an integral part of Native American culture and beliefs, so it would make sense to see one of these animals. The tree was directly behind the mist.

Photo 6 - Anomaly in top right portion of photograph

Photo 7 shows some bizarre ghostly images. People who have seen this photograph see a myriad of faces throughout the ghostly mist. Once again, the strange thing is, in the five photographs shown, the tree is always in the background or very close to the anomalies. Photos 2 and 7 are perfect examples of this. Over 150 photographs were taken that night and only these five photographs had anything strange in them.

There were some very strange happenings during that night back in November 2005. The unusual photographs, Kathy's vision during the séance and myself being pushed. My attitude toward

Photo 7 - Anomalies throughout the photograph

investigating outdoor locations has since changed. I still wonder to this day what pushed me that night. I'm not 100% sure I was pushed by the ghost or spirit of some long deceased Native American warrior. Could it have been psychokinetic energy, the act of moving an object with one's mind, that pushed me? Could Kathy have concentrated so hard on the vision that she actually caused me to be pushed using just her mind, or was I, in fact, pushed by the spirit of a Native American warrior who still found the area sacred to him? When I spoke with Kathy about the possibility of psychokinesis, she laughed and replied, "If it was psychokinesis, you would be pushed around more than just that once!" She's probably right! I may never know what happened that night, but this experience is something I will never forget.

Chapter Three

GHOSTS ALONG THE MISSISSIPPI

HAUNTED MANSIONS AND HOTELS

The Lemp Mansion

St. Louis, Missouri, the "Gateway to the West," home of the Gateway Arch, St. Louis Cardinals, Anheuser-Busch Brewery and the historic and haunted Lemp Mansion. The Lemp Mansion is situated right across Interstate 55 from the Anheuser-Busch Brewery, which is a perfect location since the Lemp family began their own brewery in 1840. In 1980, *LIFE Magazine* named the Lemp Mansion as one of the top 10 most haunted locations in America[10]. That article was written a long time ago, but if there is one place that should be haunted, it is definitely the Lemp Mansion, as we shall see from its sad and tragic history.

The original Lemp family brewery, Western Brewery[11], was started by Johann "Adam" Lemp around 1840-1842 and was the most successful of the 40 breweries in St. Louis at the time. By 1850, it was one of the largest breweries in St. Louis.

Adam Lemp passed away in August 1862 and his son, William J. Lemp Sr. took over the brewery. He continued running the Western Brewery until 1892, when the William J. Lemp Brewing Company was born out of the Western Brewery. The new stockholders elected William Sr. as president of the newly formed brewery, his son

William (Billy) Jr. as vice-president and still yet another son Louis as superintendent.

The 33-room Lemp Mansion[12] (photo 8) was constructed in 1868 by Jacob Feickert, William's father-in-law. William Sr. and his wife Julia purchased the mansion in 1876 and moved in that same year.

Photo 8 – The Lemp Mansion

Even though the mansion was magnificent at the time, William Sr. immediately went to work expanding and renovating his new home. One of the main reasons why the Lemp Mansion is so haunted is the number of suicides that have taken place inside its walls. All in all, there were three suicides that occurred inside the mansion. Three suicides, all from one family, in the same house? Either the family was cursed or the mansion was.

William Lemp Sr.[13] became despondent and withdrawn over the death of his son Frederick who passed away mysteriously in 1901. Frederick was being groomed as the heir to the company after his father when he died of an apparent heart attack at the young age of 28. William Sr. was also grieving the death of his best friend, which occurred on January 1, 1904. On the morning of February 13, 1904, William Lemp Sr., feeling downhearted and not caring anymore about family, friends and life, went into his second-floor bedroom inside the mansion, put a gun to his head and pulled the trigger. He was 68 years old. This was the first suicide inside the mansion that tragically struck the Lemp family, but it would not be the last.

After William Sr.'s death, his son "Billy" Jr.[14] took over the company in November 1904.

In the 1910s the Lemp Brewery started to suffer due to the threat of prohibition on the horizon. The brewery was not able to sustain itself financially, eventually ceasing production for good in 1920. All of the buildings and property were sold at auction to the International Shoe Company. Billy Jr., distraught over the fall of the family empire and a divorce in 1909, in which he lost custody of his only son, followed in his father's footsteps. On December 29, 1922, Billy went into his office inside the mansion, put a gun to his chest and pulled the trigger. Billy Jr. was 55 years old. Today, that room is a first-floor dining room at the northwest corner of the mansion.

Twenty-seven years later on May 10, 1949, Charles Lemp[15], who never married and was the third son of William Lemp Sr., committed suicide inside the mansion by putting a gun to his head. Prior to killing himself, he shot and killed his pet dog. Charles was the only one to leave a suicide note, which read, "In case I am found dead, blame it on no one but me." He was 77.

Another Lemp suicide that did not occur inside the mansion happened on March 20, 1920, when Elsa Lemp Wright[16], the youngest daughter of William Sr., killed herself with a gun while lying in her bed inside the St. Louis home she shared with her husband. She and her husband were divorced in 1919, but reconciled and remarried in March 1920, several weeks before she killed herself.

As if all the suicides weren't enough, there is a strange story surrounding the Lemp family concerning the "Monkey-face boy,"[17] who is said to have lived in the attic. Legend has it that Billy Lemp fathered an illegitimate son who was born with Down Syndrome. Zeke, as he was known, was "locked" away in the attic, which was also the servants' quarters, where family members and servants cared for him. The legend goes that when he was 16 years old, Zeke died as a result of a fall down the attic stairs.

What the hell was going on with the Lemp family? Were they cursed? How could a father and three of his adult children commit suicide like that? The fact is, these deaths are not stories verbally passed down. These were actually documented sad and tragic deaths that occurred within this family and in this one particular house. I hope you can now appreciate and understand why the Lemp Mansion is regarded as one of the most haunted locations in America.

Just like other well-known haunted locations, this is one place I definitely wanted to investigate, and since my sister lived in Missouri, it was surely going to happen.

In August 2007, my wife and I decided to pay a visit to my sister in Moberly, Missouri. We brought our bicycles on this trip because we wanted to bike along the Mississippi River. I researched and discovered the MCT Confluence Trail along the east side of the Mississippi that starts in Alton, Illinois and ends 18.7 miles away in Granite City, Illinois. This was also a perfect time for us to spend a night at the Lemp Mansion. So, off we went with our bicycles and paranormal equipment en route to Missouri.

After spending a week with my sister and her family in Moberly, Kathy and I headed to St. Louis and the Lemp Mansion. We arrived at the mansion in the early afternoon and even though it was situated in a busy part of St. Louis and right next to the interstate, it still looked intimidating and spooky at the same time. Painted on the side of the three-story mansion, facing the parking lot and prominently facing the interstate, is a blue, gold and white painted mural that reads "Historic Lemp Mansion Restaurant and Inn Lunch – Dinner – Banquets" (photo 9). There is also an image of a man pouring a bottle of beer into a glass. The brick in the front and south side of the mansion is painted white.

Photo 9 – The Lemp Mansion

We went inside and checked into our room. We booked the Lavender Suite, which was located on the second floor, overlooking the parking lot and the interstate. Our room, located at the top of the stairs on the left, was huge, running almost the whole length of the mansion and consisted of a large sitting/dining room, bedroom and a large bathroom, which was almost as large as the bedroom itself. The room is named after Billy Jr.'s ex-wife Lillian Handlan Lemp who was known in St. Louis society as the "Lavender Lady" because she dressed exclusively in lavender dresses.

After settling in, we explored the building and grounds. Much of the once-grand grounds are now squeezed into a tiny section of DeMenil Place near the Benton Park area of St. Louis. Outside to the right of the mansion is a tent and gazebo where ceremonies and receptions are held. I like to walk around a historical property like the Lemp Mansion to try and feel what it was like in its glorious past. What were the people like? What were the smells common to the property? Was it a bustling place with people coming and going or was it a calmer atmosphere with people going about their daily business without a care in the world?

After exploring, we decided to eat dinner in the Lemp Mansion Restaurant. It was then that we discovered we would be the only guests in the mansion. Wow, this was getting better by the minute! We would virtually have the whole place to ourselves to conduct our investigation.

After a delicious meal, we gathered our investigative gear and waited for the sun to go down before starting out. We began our investigation on the first floor in the dining room and back hallway armed with EMF meters, audio recorders, a video camera and a digital camera. Kathy was using the audio recorder and the EMF meter. I had a digital camera and the video camera on a tripod. Whenever we entered a different room, I would place the video camera in a strategic area that captured most of that particular room. I would then start snapping photographs while Kathy conducted EVP sessions on her audio recorder. We stayed in the dining area for a while and then moved toward the front rooms. We entered the former office of Billy Jr., the same room in which he killed himself almost 85 years earlier. What an uneasy feeling knowing you are in the same room where someone took their own life. Kathy stayed in the former office, which was now a private dining area, continuing her EVP session (photo 10) while I stepped out into the main hallway near the staircase. While I was exploring the hallway and

snapping photographs, I heard a man's voice whisper into my ear, "Hey." At first, I thought it was Kathy, so I said, "What?" She replied, "What?" I replied back, "You just called me. What do you need?" She stated she never called out to me. At that point, I realized it

Photo 10 – Kathy investigating the private dining area

was a disembodied voice and there was something else in the hallway with me, causing the hair on the back of my neck to stand up. It could not have been anyone else in the building, because we were the only ones there.

We investigated the rest of the first floor and then went up to the second floor, where we continued investigating for several more hours, including the area of the stairs where Zeke allegedly fell to his death. There were no other paranormal experiences, so we called it a night. The next day we would be biking along the Mississippi and then heading home.

We had no other experiences during our stay, except for that incident with the whisper in my ear. Most of the time during an investigation, you never capture anything or have any experiences, so we were very happy with this visit, especially since we were able to investigate the famous Lemp Mansion.

I would recommend the Lemp Mansion for all paranormal enthusiasts. The inn is an outstanding place to stay and the food is very good. There is also a lot to see and do in the area, including the Anheuser-Busch Brewery, the St. Louis Gateway Arch, historic St. Charles, Missouri, and the most haunted small town in America, Alton, Illinois, which we will be talking about next.

The Lemp mansion has been featured on *MTV's FEAR*, *Off Limits*, *Ghost Hunters*, *Ghost Lab*, *Most Terrifying Places in America 2*, *Ghost Adventures* and *Paranormal Witness*.

Lemp Mansion
3322 DeMenil Place
St. Louis, Missouri 63118
Phone: 314-664-8024
Website: www.lempmansion.com

The McPike Mansion

Alton, Illinois, was originally developed as a river town in 1818 and is situated some 15 miles north of St. Louis, Missouri, along the mighty Mississippi River. Alton is considered by many to be one of the most haunted small towns in all of America[18]. The population in 2010 according to the U.S. Census was 27,865,[19] a decline of just over 35% from its peak population of just over 43,000 people in 1960. Alton is considered part of the Metro East region of the Greater St. Louis metropolitan area and is noted for several historical facts, besides being named one of the most haunted towns in America. What caused the city to lose its population? Is it so haunted that people cannot live there?

Alton was home to Robert Pershing Wadlow[20] (February 22, 1918-July 15, 1940) who is listed in the *Guinness Book of World Records* as the tallest known person to have ever lived. He grew to an astounding 8 feet 11.1 inches and weighed 439 pounds! When Robert was 10 years old, he weighed 210 pounds and stood 6 feet 5 inches! He was still growing at the time of his death when he was 22 years old. Robert is buried in Oakwood Cemetery in Upper Alton, Illinois.

Alton was an important stop on the Underground Railroad. Many of the homes in Alton were equipped with hidden tunnels and secret hiding places where slaves fleeing from the south were kept hidden on their treacherous journey north to freedom. Slave catchers and pro-slavery activists from the pro-slavery state of Missouri just across the river would constantly raid Alton in search of runaway slaves.

Alton was also home to the first penitentiary in Illinois, which was constructed in 1833. It was closed in 1860 when a new prison was constructed in Joliet, Illinois. Think "Joliet" Jake Blues from the 1980 comedy "*The Blues Brothers.*" In 1862, the prison became known as the Alton Federal Military Prison[21] and was used to house Confederate prisoners during the American Civil War. Over the next three years, the prison held some 12,000 Confederate prisoners. A smallpox epidemic in 1863-1864 claimed the lives of an estimated 1,500-2,200 prisoners. Those unlucky southern prisoners would never see their homes or loved ones again. They were all buried in a mass grave on the north side of Alton.

But what makes Alton so haunted? Could it be its violent history that included murder, war, death and destruction? Could it be the limestone the town is built over or the many homes built with limestone? One of the many things Alton is famous for is the limestone bluffs along the Mississippi River just north of the city. Many believe that limestone can retain the psychic impression of past events. Could these be some of the reasons people packed up and moved from Alton or is there something more sinister going on?

There are numerous haunted locations in and around Alton, including the First Unitarian Church, the Confederate prison, the Mineral Springs Hotel, the Milton School and the subject of this chapter, the McPike Mansion.

The famous McPike Mansion[22] (photo 11) was built in 1869 for Henry Guest McPike and his family. McPike, an avid

Photo 11 - The McPike Mansion

horticulturalist, named the estate, which consisted of 15 acres of land, Point Lookout because it was situated on one of the highest points in Alton. The McPike Mansion is located almost 22 miles, as the crow flies, due north of the Lemp Mansion. The three-story brick mansion, designed by architect Lucas Pfeiffenberger (1834-1918), is of the Italianate, Second Empire architectural style that was prevalent in America from the 1840s to the 1890s and consists of 16 rooms with 11 marble fireplaces and a vaulted wine cellar. According to the McPike Mansion website, the McPike family lived in the mansion until 1936. Various owners occupied the mansion into the 1950s when it was abandoned and left empty and neglected. Why would someone abandon a grand old mansion like the McPike? It makes one wonder why, and since this book is about the paranormal, could it be the mansion was left uninhabited because of, do I dare say the word – ghosts? There are many people, including psychics and mediums, who believe the old mansion is haunted by the previous owners. The wine cellar in the basement is said to be one of the most active areas inside the mansion, with visitors and ghost hunters alike hearing footsteps and voices. There are also reports of a ghostly mist that will follow people around from room to room in the basement. The rest of the once-grand mansion is just as haunted, with an apparition of a man being seen, as well as the sounds of footsteps, the sensation of being touched and objects mysteriously disappearing, only to reappear in another area of the mansion.

I watched an episode about the McPike Mansion on one of the many paranormal television shows I used to watch. I was always looking for places to investigate and this one was perfect, since, like the Lemp Mansion, it was on the drive from my home in Ohio to my sister's home in Missouri.

In June 2011, Kathy and I traveled to Alton, Illinois, to investigate the McPike Mansion. My sister Shelley and her husband Jim decided to meet us for this investigation. We booked a room several miles up the Mississippi River at a little hotel in Grafton, Illinois, called the Ruebel Hotel that is said to be haunted. We will talk about the Ruebel Hotel later in this chapter.

Prior to investigating the McPike, I contacted the owner Sharyn Luedke for permission to investigate the property. She was very gracious and gave us permission to investigate the exterior of the mansion. Due to construction and unsafe conditions inside the mansion, we would not be able to investigate the interior. That was okay with me; I was just happy to investigate any part of this historic mansion and its grounds. Please remember to ALWAYS obtain permission to investigate ANY private property and NEVER trespass after hours without permission from the property owner or someone authorized to give permission. I cannot stress this enough. You don't want to give paranormal investigators a bad name and better yet, you don't want to be arrested and thrown in jail for trespassing.

We arrived in the late evening, parked at the end of the driveway and checked in with the owner, who lived next door. Holy crap did this place look creepy and haunted! If you ever imagined what a haunted house should look like, this was it. Now I'm glad we weren't able to go inside. This place could easily be used for any haunted house or murder house in any type of horror movie. Here you go, James Wan -- the perfect filming location!

We walked back to our car, retrieved a digital camera, EMF meter and a digital audio recorder and then proceeded to walk up the driveway to the front of the mansion. The front of the mansion, including the porch running the entire width, seemed to be in pretty

decent shape. The sides and the back of the mansion, however, were a different story, with windows boarded over, rotting wood and deteriorating porches, along with overgrown shrubs and trees. There is a lot of work to be done to restore the mansion to its former

Photo 12 - The McPike Mansion

self and the Luedkes are working very hard in its restoration. Sharyn and her husband George Luedke have been slowly returning the mansion to its former glory through donations and tours. In 2017, the Alton Historical Commission presented them with an award in preservation for work done on the front porch and conservatory.

We walked around the mansion and the grounds, taking photographs and stopping every so often to conduct an EVP session using the audio recorder.

All of us sat on the front porch listening to the sounds of the night, hoping for something to happen...except Jim who is non-believer. After several hours of roaming the property, we decided it was time to leave. Kathy wanted to conduct one last EVP session in front of the house just off the porch. I was still sitting on the porch and Shelley and Jim went back to the car to wait for us to finish. Kathy was wearing earphones to listen in real time. The nice thing about listening in real time is you can hear potential EVPs as they happen. You don't have to go back and listen to everything again in the hopes you might have captured something. During the EVP session (photo 13), Kathy stated, "If you don't mind, I am going to go sit on your front porch." Almost immediately, Kathy heard through the earphones what sounded like a woman saying, "I don't mind."

Kathy immediately called me over so I could listen too. I heard a faint voice saying what sounded like "I don't mind." At the time, there were only the two of us in front of the mansion and I did not hear anyone other than Kathy talking.

Photo 13 - Kathy doing an EVP session

It was a nice night and the property was a cool place to wander around, but we didn't see any ghosts staring out of any windows, nor did we capture anything in all of the photographs taken, but we did record that one possible EVP.

We thanked Sharyn for her hospitality and left to head back to our hotel, but we were not finished investigating. We still wanted to investigate the Ruebel Hotel.

The McPike Mansion has been featured on *Scariest Places on Earth* and *Fact or Faked: Paranormal Files* and is listed on the National Register of Historic Places.

McPike Mansion
2018 Alby Street
Alton, Illinois 62002
Website: www.mcpikemansion.com

The Ruebel Hotel

The Ruebel Hotel (photo 14) in Grafton, Illinois, is approximately 17 miles up the Mississippi River from Alton. We chose to stay here during our trip to Alton because we knew this hotel had a reputation for being haunted.

Grafton[23] was founded in 1832 by James Mason and was given the name Grafton after Mason's birthplace of Grafton, Massachusetts.

Photo 14 - The Ruebel Hotel

Grafton was a booming town in the middle of the 19th century due to its location on the Mississippi River and its surrounding stone quarries. Because Grafton is situated on the river, boat building and commercial fishing were big industries. In the 1850s, Grafton's population was around 10,000 people, but has since dwindled to 674 residents, according to the 2010 census.

The current Ruebel Hotel[24] was built in 1913 and is the second hotel constructed on that site after the original one, built in 1879, burned down in 1912. The original hotel had 32 rooms and was a major stopping location for travelers on the Mississippi River. In 1984, the hotel was abandoned and would stay that way until 1997 when the building was purchased, renovated and opened again for business. The Ruebel Hotel was named after Michael Ruebel, the original owner.

The Ruebel has its share of ghost stories with the most prominent one of a little girl named "Abigail." She has been known to run up and down the stairs and hallway during the early morning hours, as well as moving and hiding small personal items. Hotel guests even claim to have seen her and spoken with her. There have also been reports of cold spots, light switches turning off by themselves, doors opening and closing, and disembodied voices. In fact, in 2011, the website Mysterious Heartland rated the Ruebel Hotel as the 10th Most Haunted Hotel in the State of Illinois[25].

Abigail[26] was a 9-year-old girl who died of cholera while traveling the Mississippi River with her family. She became too ill to travel, so her family decided to leave her at the hotel until she recovered. Cholera

Photo 15 - The Rubel Hotel lobby

is an often-fatal bacterial disease that is contracted through consuming infected water or food, especially undercooked seafood, which can cause severe vomiting, cramping and diarrhea. If it is left untreated, death can occur within hours. Unfortunately, Abigail never recovered from her disease and died in the hotel…or so it has been told.

Once we returned to the Ruebel Hotel, Kathy, Shelley and I went right to work preparing for our investigation. Jim decided he had enough investigating for the night and retired to the Family/Apartment Suite located on the lower floor where we were staying.

We started our investigation by conducting an EVP session on the stairs leading to the second floor. We placed an EMF meter on the stairs in the hope we would receive some type of electrical energy that could indicate possible paranormal activity. With no luck on the stairs, we headed down to the banquet room (photo 16) where we repeated the same process. Again, we captured nothing indicative of

any paranormal activity. Since it was now getting extremely late, we decided to call it quits and retire for the night.

The Ruebel Hotel is listed on the National Register of Historic Places and currently has 22 rooms, as well as a bar and restaurant. It is said that

Photo 16 - Shelley and Kathy investigating the banquet room

room #11, the Sultana room, is the room with the most activity. Some say this is the room in which Abigail died.

Ruebel Hotel
217 East Main Street
Grafton, Illinois 62037
Phone: 618-786-2315
Website: www.ruebelhotel.com.

Photo 17 - The Ruebel Hotel bar

Chapter Four

A HAUNTED MOBILE HOME

SNEAKERS AT PLAY AGAIN

When my parents got older, they decided it was time to sell their house and move into a resort campground where they could live out their final years in peace, relaxation and enjoyment.

Growing up, I remember both of my parents loved camping. Just about every "vacation" I went on as a young teenager was centered around camping and boating. We originally started camping in a tent, which as a young boy was very exciting to me. We then added a rowboat to our camping trips so we could go fishing. My parents eventually got tired of tent camping; too much work setting up and breaking down, and purchased a pickup truck with a small camper in the bed. They got rid of the rowboat; too much work there, also, and purchased a motorboat. Camping equipment and the way we camped kept improving, until it all got too much for them. My parents finally purchased a membership in a private campground where they could keep their camper trailer all year long. I'm not complaining at all, as I used to have a blast on these weekend "getaways"! The majority of the time, we went with other family members and enjoyed hiking, swimming, boating and water skiing. I have wonderful and fond memories of these mini vacations.

It was no surprise to me when, in 1997, they sold their house in Canton and purchased a lot with a permanent camper trailer and moved into a private resort campground in East Sparta, Ohio. The campground had everything you could want, including a swimming lake, fishing lake, in-ground pool and clubhouse, where numerous activities and events were held throughout the summer months. I used to take my children there and we would have a blast swimming and driving around in my parents' golf cart. The only problem with moving into a resort campground in Northern Ohio was it was only open from April until October due to the fine weather. If you don't like the weather in Northeast Ohio, wait a day or two and it will change at a moment's notice. One day the high will be 40 degrees; the next day it will be 75!

My parents needed another option for the winter months so they purchased a mobile home in Moberly, Missouri, to be closer to my sister, Shelley. If you read my first book, "*Insights into the Unknown: A Ghost Hunter's Journey,*" you may remember my sister's haunted house in Moberly. Moving to Missouri during the winter months?!? What were they thinking?!? I'm not saying anything bad about the good people of Missouri and Moberly, but your winters are no better than Ohio's. Why didn't they move somewhere like Florida? Then I would have had a place to stay when I visited Walt Disney World, "the happiest place on earth" and one of my favorite vacation spots in the world!

My parents only stayed in Missouri for about three years before deciding to move back to Ohio in 1999. I guess they missed me and probably liked me more than my sister! Sorry, Shelley!

After returning to Ohio, my parents confided in me -- when they were living in their mobile home in Missouri, they believed it to be haunted. Haunted? My parents thought their mobile home was haunted? To hear that coming from my dad, who didn't believe in ghosts or anything paranormal or unknown for that matter, was quite a shock. Dad and I used to get into lengthy discussions about ghosts, UFOs and aliens. He would make me so frustrated because I could not convince him otherwise. As my wife Kathy says, like father like son! Dad always thought there were logical explanations for ghostly experiences, but even he was stumped by some of the events that he experienced in their Missouri home.

Both of my parents said personal belongings would often disappear, and they would sometimes hear footsteps as if someone were walking around the mobile home. They would even hear knocks on the front door, but no one would be there when they would answer. One of the strangest stories they relayed was that of Dad's missing gold chain necklace. Dad told me the following story, which I find all the more credible because he didn't believe in anything.

One evening, he placed his gold chain necklace on his dresser before going to bed like he always did. When he woke up the next morning, Dad went to put on the chain, but it was gone. Both he and Mom searched the home thoroughly, but the chain was nowhere to be found. They were dumbfounded. Dad did not believe it was paranormal at the time, but he could not explain how the chain had disappeared. Dad gave up on ever finding the chain again, when one day, about a month later, it reappeared on the floor in the middle of their bedroom. It was neatly coiled in a perfect circle in plain view! They had no idea how the chain came to be in the middle of their floor -- the area they had walked by hundreds of times and even vacuumed numerous times since the necklace had gone missing. Maybe they didn't miss me after all and moved back to Ohio because their mobile home was haunted! Oh well, the thought was nice while it lasted.

After my parents moved back to Ohio, they eventually purchased another mobile home in Fohl Village, a trailer park located just a short distance away from their private summer campground. This would be their new winter home.

Those three years of living in Missouri gave my dad a more open mind on the paranormal and he now was genuinely curious and interested in it. It looks like living in a haunted house and having experiences of his own changed his mind when I couldn't. Isn't that how these things happen? Skeptics and non-believers are never believers until one day it happens to them. After Dad's experiences, after I would return from an investigation, he would always ask what happened and if we had captured any evidence. He started listening to the EVPs we recorded and was amazed at some of the voices that seemed to speak out from beyond the grave. Dad never even tried to come up with any logical explanations for the EVPs -- he now was a true believer.

The mobile home they purchased in Fohl Village was actually pretty nice. Once you entered the side (main) door, you were in the living room. To the right was a short hall that led to my dad's full bathroom and his office/bedroom. To the left of the main door through the living room was a small dining area, kitchen, laundry room, Mom's bedroom and her full bathroom. I think when I'm ready, I'll purchase a nice mobile home to live my final years in, but I think I'll find one where it's a little bit warmer…maybe down south somewhere.

Things were pretty quiet in their new home, paranormally speaking, until one of their beloved cats passed away. Then strange things started to happen. Mom was a cat lover and always had at least one as a pet. In their private campground, she was known as the "Cat Lady" because she would always take care of the stray cats in the campground. She was not a cat hoarder, but genuinely cared about "her cats" welfare. She always had food out for them and would fix up places for them to stay warm while they were outside. She would not keep them, but would instead try to capture them in carriers to take them to the local Humane Society. She always worried about "her cats" and took great care of them whenever she could. In the winter months when the campground was closed, she would make special trips there to make sure they had food and shelter.

Photo 18 - Sneakers

One of Mom's favorite cats was a stray she kept as a pet, named Sneakers. Sneakers (photo 18) was a yellow tabby mix with a scaredy-cat-type of personality. I rarely saw Sneakers when I visited my parents, as he would bolt for his favorite hiding place and would not come out until after I left. Now I know where the phrase "scaredy-cat" comes from.

Mom and Dad loved Sneakers and were devastated when he passed away in early 2008. They were so devastated, they had Sneakers cremated and kept his ashes in a tin in Mom's bedroom. This is the first time I saw my parents do anything like that, even though they had several pets in the past. The first pet we owned was a mutt named Penny because his coat was a shiny copper color. Penny could be ornery at times, but was a fun dog to play with. He always had his "blanket" with him, carrying it everywhere with it hanging out of his mouth and dragging behind him. His blanket was usually an old pair of pants or jeans that he liked to rip apart. He must have gone through about a thousand blankets in his lifetime! My sister Shelley and I used to tease him all the time by taking his blanket and hiding it throughout the house. It was fun to watch him go crazy trying to find it, which he always did. In those days we didn't have cable, video games, cell phones or the internet to keep us amused…Penny was our daily entertainment!

After 14 years, our beloved Penny passed away in 1978. In 1980, my parents got another dog, Max, part Labrador Retriever who just loved the water. Instead of a blanket like Penny used to have, Max had his little yellow rubber "hamburger" that was always sticking out the side of his mouth. I loved taking Max to a local park with a creek and waterfalls for him to play in. On the drive to the park, Max would have his head hanging out the car window, just like dogs' love to do, with that damn hamburger in his mouth. He would occasionally drop it out the window and we would have to turn around to go back to retrieve it. Max would get extremely excited when we arrived at the park because he knew he was going to get to play in the water. As soon as I would open the door, he would knock me over to get out of the car and then race down the hill to the creek and start splashing around. I would throw the hamburger off the waterfall, and Max would leap from the top into the water to go after his precious hamburger! It was always a fun and special time together at the park.

I also taught Max how to climb a tree by placing his hamburger between tree trunks. Max learned to climb up the tree to get it down. Max was a cool dog and I loved him like he was my own.

Prior to Sneaker's passing, my parents got another cat, which they just called Kitty (photo 19). Clever name! Kitty was all black, with white paws and a white chest and, just like Sneakers, was a scaredy-cat. Whenever I would visit them, Kitty would be nowhere to be found. In all the times I visited, I rarely saw her.

Photo 19 - Kitty

I know, I know, I've talked too much about pets and not enough about ghosts and hauntings, but I am getting there.

After Sneakers passed away, strange things soon began to happen in my parents' mobile home. On several occasions, they would hear meowing coming from Mom's bedroom, the same bedroom where Sneakers slept and where his ashes were kept, even though Kitty was sitting with them on the couch.

In August 2008, my mom had open heart surgery and my sister Shelley came in from Missouri to help her and Dad, who was also extremely sick at the time with heart disease.

One night, Shelley was staying in the mobile home while Mom and Dad stayed at the campground. There wasn't much room in the camper for others to sleep, as there was only one small bedroom in the camper trailer. There wasn't even a full-sized couch in the camper, just a love seat and a couple of rocking chairs in the small living room. Shelley stated she was lying on Mom's bed (photo 20) in her bedroom watching television when she heard what sounded like a cat meowing from inside the room. Shelley froze in fear with the hairs at the back of her neck standing up. She knew it wasn't Kitty because she was at the camper with Mom and Dad. Shelley also knew it wasn't coming from outside the bedroom because the meowing came from the foot of the bed! Just then, Shelley felt something jump onto the foot of the bed and start walking toward her! She felt a weight on her body, as whatever was on the bed was walking on *her* toward her head! She screamed and yelled at it to get down, which, for Shelley's sake, it did! Needless to say, she had a hard time sleeping that night and opted to keep both the television and the light on!

When Shelley told Mom what happened, Mom said that she hears Sneakers all the time and he will also jump onto the bed with her.

Photo 20 - Mom's bedroom

"Thanks for the heads-up, Mom! Wish you would have told me sooner!"

In December 2008, Shelley and Mom had another experience with Sneakers. They were sitting on the living room sofa, watching television with Kitty between them, when they both heard a loud meow coming from the center of the living room. Kitty heard it too and lifted her head up to see where the "other" cat was. Both Shelley and Mom looked at each other, knowing that Sneakers was in the room with them!

In September 2008, at the age of 73, my father passed away in his bedroom (photo 21) in the mobile home after a short illness. He had recently entered hospice care and was now living out the remainder of his life in his bedroom at home. I visited him the evening before he passed. Dad didn't want me to leave, but I had to work the next morning and my parents lived over an hour away. Just as I arrived

Photo 21 – Dad's bedroom

at work the next morning, I received a phone call from my wife Kathy who told me Mom had just called to say Dad passed away during the night. I was devastated, not because Dad had passed -- we were expecting it and I didn't want to see him in pain anymore. I was devastated because I did not stay when he asked me to. I think he knew he was not going to make it through the night and wanted me, his only son, to be with him when he passed. He didn't want to die alone. I remember thinking how he finally has all the answers to life's mysteries that he didn't have when he was alive.

After Dad passed away, Mom started having more strange encounters in the home that could not be attributed to Sneakers.

Mom was lying in bed one evening shortly after Dad's passing, watching television, when she heard the cabinet door in the laundry room open and then slam shut. The sudden and loud noise startled her and caused Kitty to jump. The walls in the home were paper thin, with the laundry room sharing a wall with her bedroom, so what she heard was very loud and distinct. Mom had put Dad's wine opener in the laundry room cabinet after he passed away. When Dad was alive, it was always kept in the dining room where it was easy for him to use. Was Dad upset that Mom had moved his wine opener into the laundry room and was showing his displeasure? Maybe Dad wanted some wine, but was upset because he couldn't find his wine opener. Sounds crazy, but is anything really that crazy when speaking of ghosts and the paranormal?

Mom also told me that doors throughout the home were always opening and closing on their own. One evening while she was lying in bed, she heard Dad's bedroom door open and close, just like it did when he was alive.

One morning, for whatever reason, Mom's alarm clock failed to go off. While still asleep, she distinctly heard Dad's voice telling her it was time to get up for work. She woke up and discovered that she had slept in. If she had not heard Dad's voice, she would have been late for work. Mom swore up and down that she wasn't dreaming and that his voice was coming from the bedroom -- just like when he was alive and telling her to get up for work.

Mom had so many strange things happening in her home she asked if I could investigate to see if Dad was still there.

On February 7th, 2009, my wife Kathy and I, along with another investigator, went to Mom's home to do an investigation. It was now a little over four months since Dad had passed away.

We brought our usual equipment consisting of video cameras, digital cameras, audio recorders and EMF detectors.

We set up three video cameras throughout the home -- one in Mom's bedroom, one in the living room and another in Dad's bedroom where he passed away.

All of us except Mom, went into Dad's bedroom to begin the investigation. Mom decided to stay in the living room in case anything happened there. During the investigation, we used a variety of devices in an attempt to capture evidence, including digital audio recorders to capture Electronic Voice Phenomenon also known as EVPs. During the EVP session in Dad's bedroom, Kathy saw the

reflection of a man's face in the glass doors of a hutch. The reflection was only there for a moment, so Kathy could not describe any features of the face other than the fact that it was wearing glasses. Dad had worn glasses for as long as I could remember (photo 22). Maybe it was Dad trying to reach out to us. After investigating his bedroom for a while longer, we moved into Mom's bedroom to continue.

Photo 22 - Dad

While we were investigating her bedroom, Mom, who was sitting in the living room said she heard noises that sounded like cabinet doors opening and closing in the kitchen. We were in her bedroom at the time with the door closed and did not hear anything coming from the kitchen. During a later review of the evidence, it was determined that what Mom heard coming from the kitchen was a bedroom chair creaking from one of the investigators sitting on it.

For the next couple of days after the investigation, we reviewed all of the evidence and nothing that could be considered paranormal, other than the face Kathy saw in the mirror and some minor "hits" on the EMF detectors, was found.

Minor things continued to happen in Mom's home, but it didn't seem to bother her. I guess she felt having them there gave her comfort and made her seem not so alone. I asked her on many occasions to move in with Kathy and me, but she always declined. I can't imagine how lonely she must have felt living alone, especially in the evening hours, after being married for over 51 years, but then I guess she always had Kitty, Sneakers and now Dad to keep her company.

In November 2013, doctors discovered a small mass of cancer on one of Mom's lungs. I was with her at her oncologist when the doctor went over her options -- leave it alone or have surgery to remove the cancer. She elected to have the surgery.

Mom had surgery the first week of December, and according to her doctor, the surgery had been successful and he expected her to make a full recovery. Mom came and stayed with Kathy and me until she was strong enough to return home. However, that wasn't to be the case. She took a turn for the worse and started to go downhill. Throughout the rest of December and January Mom was in and out of the emergency room, hospital and a rehabilitation home.

One night while we were all sleeping, Kathy woke with a panicked feeling. She bolted up in bed and thought something was wrong with Mom. She went upstairs and discovered Mom trying to get out of bed to go to the bathroom. Mom had a walker, but was so weak she could barely walk with it. As Kathy helped her to the bathroom, Mom asked, "Who were all those people in the bedroom causing all that noise?" There was no one else in the house. Could it be long-deceased relatives and friends celebrating in anticipation of Mom being reunited with them soon?

On January 30th, 2014, mom finally lost her fight and passed away peacefully in a hospital room. Kathy, my sister Shelley and I were with her when she passed. Now she was finally with Dad again. Strange as it may seem, but it was a peaceful time for all of us and we were relieved that she didn't have to suffer anymore.

Since I was the executor, I had to take care of all of her personal and financial affairs, which included selling her mobile home and camper trailer, and dividing and removing all of her personal belongings from both places.

One Saturday afternoon in late February 2014, Kathy, our daughter-in-law Tina, our three-and-a-half-year-old grandson Connor and I went to Mom's mobile home to go through her belongings. As we entered the front door, Connor got really excited and yelled "Kitty!" and ran into Mom's bedroom. We really didn't think anything of it at the time since our minds were preoccupied with other things. After a short time, Connor came out of the bedroom almost looking like he had seen a ghost! He slowly walked up to his mom and said, "Something freaky just happened." We asked him what happened and he took us into Mom's bathroom (photo 23) located off her bedroom. He said he was sitting on the edge of the bathtub when something furry rubbed up against his leg. He must have really seen Sneakers when we first walked into the home! He seemed really scared at the time and the strange thing is, being a little over three-years-old, he had no idea that the house was haunted by a ghost cat! We asked Connor what color the cat was and he replied that it was yellow. Understand that Connor had never seen a yellow cat before, only black ones, as family members seem to only have black cats, including his great aunt and me. It would seem that Connor really did see Sneakers.

After several months, I finally sold both the camper trailer and Mom's mobile home. Mom loved Sneakers so much that she requested his ashes be buried with her. I doubt if Dad or Sneakers ever returned to the mobile home again now that they were all happy being together again.

But what of Kitty? Mom asked Kathy and I if we could take care of her, which of course we said yes. Sometimes Kitty would sit in the living room and stare up into the loft area on the second floor, the area where Mom spent parts of December and January with us prior to her passing. Is Mom up there looking down on us to make sure we're okay? Maybe she is, because when our 12-month-old granddaughter Emma comes over, she will sit in the living room, look up into the loft, smile and wave.

Photo 23 - Mom's bathroom

Chapter Five

NORTH OLMSTED, OHIO

A SUBURBAN HAUNTING

You don't have to live in a really old house that looks like something out of a horror movie for strange and scary things to happen. You don't have to live out in the country, miles from the city for ghostly sounds to occur. Hauntings can occur anywhere. This is what Brad and Lori[*] found out when they moved into their suburban home in North Olmsted in October 1995.

Their new home was a 2,052-square-foot, two-story colonial built in 1964 on a quiet, residential street in the City of North Olmsted, Ohio. The home consisted of a living room, dining room, kitchen, family room and a half bathroom on the first floor and four bedrooms and two full bathrooms on the second floor. There was also a finished basement and an attached two-car garage.

By looking at their modest home from the outside, you would never guess there were strange happenings occurring within the walls. Who would think paranormal activities could occur in a modern home barely 45 years old? When most of us think of haunted locations, we usually have the image of an old, creepy mansion, some 100 years old, a dark, eerie cemetery or even a newer house where a murder, suicide or some other tragic event occurred. None of that was the case here.

---

[*] Names changed

The City of North Olmsted[27] was founded in 1826 and is located within Cuyahoga County, approximately 12 miles southwest of Cleveland. The city is named for Aaron Olmsted, a wealthy sea captain who purchased the land in 1806 for $30,000.

According to the 2010 census, the population of North Olmsted was 32,718, making it the 8th most populated city in Cuyahoga County and the 42nd largest city in Ohio.

North Olmsted is a shoppers' paradise with a wide variety of retail shopping areas, including Great Northern Mall, which opened in 1976. There are countless stores, restaurants, specialty shops and strip malls up and down Lorain and Brookpark roads, the main thoroughfares.

When Brad, Lori and their two young children Amy, age 8, and Brad Jr.*, age 4, moved into the home in 1995, they had no idea what would occur in their new home.

Brad was a down-to-earth, hard-working husband and father, who at times worked two jobs to support his family.

Lori was a stay-at-home mom who worked side jobs to help make ends meet, as life was financially difficult for them in the beginning. However, they were both very happy and proud of what they had accomplished in their young lives so far.

Things were pretty quiet for the family for a long time after they moved in. In fact, they lived in their home for about 13 years, when for unknown reasons, unexplained and frightening things started to happen.

---

* Names changed

One of the first occurrences happened late one night when Brad Jr., who was 18 years of age at the time, was watching television from the floor in the living room. Brad and Lori had already gone to bed for the night, leaving Brad Jr. alone in the living room. Brad Jr. eventually fell asleep on the floor and later woke up with a gripping fear that overwhelmed him. He became terrified and ran upstairs in a very emotional state. He frantically woke up his parents to explain what happened, but it was very difficult for him because even he didn't understand what he was feeling. All three of them proceeded downstairs into the living room, but could find no rational explanation of what had caused Brad Jr. to experience the terrified feelings.

Oftentimes, doors throughout the home would be found open, even though they had been previously closed. This would happen several times with the sliding glass door in the family room that led to the backyard and the refrigerator and freezer doors in the kitchen. One morning, Brad and Lori woke up and discovered both the refrigerator and freezer doors open. When they asked Brad Jr. if he left the doors open by mistake during the night, he stated no. If it wasn't anyone in the family, what could have caused both refrigerator doors to be left open? Do ghosts get hungry for a late-night snack in the middle of the night?

Both Brad and Lori stated objects would be moved or go missing altogether for a short period of time. On one occasion, stuffed animals that were kept on the spare bed in an upstairs bedroom would be found scattered in the hallway. Decorative pine cones that were displayed in baskets on the stairs to the second floor would constantly and mysteriously fall down the steps.

One day, Lori was working in the kitchen when a paper receipt that was sitting on the kitchen counter flew up into the air, as if a strong wind came, but according to Lori, there were no open windows and no breeze whatsoever in the kitchen.

The family would also hear footsteps in the house whenever they were in the rec room in the basement. They said it would sound like someone was walking around on the first floor. Several times they thought an intruder had broken into the house, but each time they would go upstairs to investigate, they would find no one in the house and all the doors and windows secured.

Brad and Lori were also having problems with the hanging light in the dining room. The light would occasionally turn on and off by itself.

One of the stranger things that happened was the disappearance of the television remote control. Brad and Lori searched all over for the remote, but no matter where they looked, they could not find it. They assumed it must have been thrown out with the trash since it was nowhere to be found. Several weeks later, Lori was in the kitchen cleaning when she heard a strange noise in the adjacent family room. She went to check and discovered the missing remote control lying in the middle of the family room floor. The noise Lori heard was apparently the remote control hitting the floor, as if it had materialized out of thin air.

The family was now starting to become unnerved by all the strange events that were happening and didn't know exactly what to do. That's when they contacted me and the paranormal team I belonged to in an effort to see if we could come up with a logical explanation of what was going on.

Prior to beginning the actual investigation, I researched the property and conducted an interview with Brad and Lori, discovering Lori's father had passed away in 2002 after a short illness. He was 74-years-old at the time of his passing. Lori also had an older sister who was 57-years-old when she passed away in August of 2008. However, neither one of them passed away in Brad and Lori's home, but that doesn't necessarily mean one of them wasn't trying to make contact or just being mischievous. Nothing else was discovered during the interview or research to explain the activity.

We conducted the investigation of the home in August 2009. Participants in the investigation included my wife Kathy, another investigator and myself.

Since it was summer, it was still daylight when we arrived at 6:00 pm. We were greeted at the door by Brad and Lori and were then given a tour of the house. They stated nothing had happened in the basement or on the second floor, except for the incident with the stuffed animals. All of the activity seemed to concentrate on the first floor. Neither Kathy, the other investigator nor I picked up any strange feelings while inside the house. Sometimes when we walk into an alleged haunted location, we can get electrically charged feelings, like pin pricks that make your hair stand up. That was not the case at this location, but that doesn't necessarily mean there isn't anything paranormal going on. It can just mean that there was nothing paranormal going on at the time we arrived.

After the initial walkthrough, we took base EMF (Electro-Magnetic Field) and temperature readings on the first floor. EMF readings seemed a little high with 3.5 mG (milligauss) readings in the kitchen, 6.5 mG in the living room and 8.2 mG in the dining room. Most private homes we investigate usually range from 0.0 mG to about 2.0 mG, with some EMF higher near certain electrical devices, but these readings were not near electrical devices or appliances. They were readings taken in the middle of the rooms. In basic terms, a milligauss is a form of measurement of the magnetic radiation field in a particular area. Everything gives off an EMF, including power lines, cell phones, refrigerators, stereo systems, microwave ovens and humans, to name just a few.

We set up three stationary video cameras and two stationary audio recorders throughout the living room and family room. At 7:05 pm, we hit record on all of the devices and left the house so the recorders could run uninterrupted for a while. We returned to the house at 8:31 pm and discovered the dining room light was turned off. The light was on when we left the house earlier, and Brad and Lori did say the light would turn off on its own. It's a good thing we had a video camera looking into the dining room so we were able to capture the light turning off.

As we were trying to figure out what caused the light to turn off, we made another EMF sweep of the house, but this time we took readings on the second floor and the basement. Readings on the second floor were in the normal range, between 0.0 mG and 0.5 mG. Readings on the first floor, specifically near the television, were now around 25.0 mG. We also checked the dining room light switch, which was located on the wall between the kitchen and dining room. We were shocked when we discovered a 40.0 mG reading at the switch! Maybe there was something wrong with the inner workings of the light switch that caused the dining room light to go on and off. That explanation made perfect sense to me and because of the high EMF coming from the switch, I don't believe the problem with the dining room light is paranormal.

A later review of the video showed the dining room light starting to flicker. After a few minutes of flickering, the light dimmed and then went off.

EMF sweeps in the basement revealed a reading of 70.0 mG coming from the wiring in the basement ceiling directly under the living room where Brad Jr. had woken up in a panic previously.

Could this high EMF that was directly under Brad Jr. be the cause of his gripping fear? Again, that made sense to me. Past studies have shown that high doses of EMF can cause a variety of health problems, including fatigue, anxiety, paranoia, depression, forgetfulness and nausea[28]. There is still ongoing scientific research to determine if high EMF can cause diseases such as cancer and Alzheimer's. For safety, the Environmental Protection Agency (EPA) recommends limiting your exposure to EMF fields to .5 mG to 2.5 mG, with 1.0 mG the preferred standard[29].

Underneath the area where Brad Jr was lying was 70.0 mG, 70x the standard recommended limit. No wonder he had that feeling of panic when he fell asleep on the floor.

Our conclusion after the investigation and reviewing all of the evidence was that bad wiring inside the home could be a contributing factor to some of the activity that was taking place. We recommended Brad and Lori seek a qualified electrician to check the wiring in their home and have it repaired if necessary.

As usual, I kept in touch with our clients for several months afterward to see how things were going. They stated they contacted an electrician and he gave them some recommendations they had not yet completed.

Things quieted down for the family for several years, but that would change in June of 2013 when Brad and Lori experienced something that was truly terrifying.

On the evening of June 6, 2013, I received a phone call from Brad who said strange and frightening things were going on in their home as we were speaking. He sounded extremely frightened as he was explaining what was happening and asked if we could come over right away. Kathy and I were only about 20 minutes away so we decided to go and see if we could help.

Kathy and I gathered some of our equipment and drove over to Brad and Lori's. We were met outside by Brad, who stated that one of the front porch lights just "blew" as he went outside to move his car.

Once inside the home, we observed one of the table lamps in the living room flickering off and on, and there was also a heaviness in the air that Kathy and I both felt.

After Brad and Lori calmed down, they told us what happened. Both of them were sitting in the living room watching television when the table lamp started flickering. Lori was sitting on the sofa and Brad was sitting on a recliner with the table between them. While the lamp was flickering, they started hearing strange noises, like something was being moved around in the basement, when all of a sudden, they heard a loud crash directly below where they were sitting! They both jumped out of their skin and their seats because it was so loud and startling. They believed someone had somehow broken into their house and was in the basement. Brad grabbed a baseball bat and they both slowly and cautiously made their way down into the basement.

They quietly proceeded down the steps into the basement, their muscles tensed and their hearts racing. They crept into the laundry room, with Brad tightly gripping the bat, ready to swing at anything or anyone and searched the area. They didn't find anyone hiding, but they did find an old 5-foot-long stair handrail lying in the middle of the laundry room floor directly under where they were sitting in the living room. Finding the handrail on the floor really frightened them and this is when they went upstairs and called me.

We all went into the basement where Brad and Lori showed us the handrail sitting in the middle of the floor. Brad explained that the handrail had been wedged up in the ceiling joists in the basement for several years. Brad believed there was no way the handrail could have come loose on its own because the brackets were still attached. Someone or something would have to lift the handrail up out of the joists and remove it.

We went back upstairs and turned our attention to the lamp on the table, which was still flickering. I thought there might be a problem with the lamp itself, so we switched light bulbs from a lamp in the family room to the lamp in the living room. This seemed to take care of the problem as both light bulbs and lamps worked normally. After about an hour we switched the light bulbs back. Again, the lamp in the living room started flickering again, so it seems that for whatever reason, probably more electrical than paranormal, that particular light bulb wasn't functioning correctly in that particular lamp.

All four of us sat in the living room discussing what was going on. We had a digital audio recorder on the coffee table recording at the time. During a later review of that audio recorder, two possible EVPs were discovered. The first one sounded like a male voice saying, "House won" or "House one." The second EVP sounded like a couple of female voices agreeing with what we were talking about, saying things like, "yea" and "uh huh."

Why and how could things like this happen? First, let's discuss the problem with the lights. The flickering light bulb in the lamp and the light that "blew" on the porch could be the result of an electrical problem in the house. As found during our first investigation, there is high EMF in the house that the owners did not correct as recommended from our first investigation. That is as good a theory as any, but there are a couple of holes. Both the problem with the table lamp and the front porch light happened at the same time, at the same moment the handrail fell in the basement and around the same time the EVPs were captured. Brad and Lori had never had problems with the lamp or front porch light prior to this evening, or since. It was almost as if a huge wave of unknown energy surged throughout the living room.

I have to admit I could not figure out how the handrail was able to come loose and fall to the floor on its own. We were able to offer only three possible explanations.

First – The handrail worked itself loose over time due to vibrations caused by people walking on the floor above. This seems highly unlikely though as the handrail was basically wedged and secured in place by the brackets.

Second – The handrail was removed from the joists by some paranormal force. Lori has suffered the loss of four members of her family in recent years. Her father passed away in 2002, her older sister passed away in 2008, her older brother passed away in 2011 and most recently, her mother passed away in May 2012 in the family room of her own home. Could it be one of them trying to get her attention for some unknown reason?

Third – The handrail was moved by psychokinetic energy. It seems that Lori had been under a great deal of stress recently due to an incident she had the previous evening with one of her neighbors. Lori was extremely frightened and worried that the neighbor was going to harm her in some way. She even stated she needed to move her family for their safety. It is a possibility that all of the activity was subconsciously caused by Lori. She was sitting next to the lamp when the lamp starting flickering and the handrail was almost directly underneath her as she sat in the living room. In fact, while we were discussing the possibility of this theory with Brad and Lori, the lamp ceased flickering.

We will never know the exact reason why things happened that evening, and whether it was natural causes, paranormal or psychokinetic as they have since moved from their home in the suburbs. I wonder if the new owners have experienced anything unusual or if they are happy in their new home?

Chapter Six

MEDINA COUNTY, OHIO

THE CASE OF THE "LADYBUG"

When you think of a ladybug, you think of a cute, small, usually red-colored beetle with black spots that we all played with as kids, or at least I did. There are certain insects that people usually do not like or are afraid of such as spiders, centipedes, bees, flies, cockroaches and mosquitoes just to name a few. But, it seems everyone loves ladybugs -- that is, until you really get to know them. Most species of ladybugs are beneficial to humans because they eat aphids that cause extensive damage to crops, however, some species of ladybugs can do just as much damage to plants and crops as aphids[30].

Another little-known fact about ladybugs is that they can bite. Have you ever been bitten by one? It must be an adult thing because, as a kid growing up, I handled a lot of ladybugs and never remembered getting bitten once. Now, as an adult, it seems every time I handle one it bites me. They don't hurt too much, but you will know when you've been bitten. The bite feels like a minor sting that can leave a mark, but since ladybugs do not deliver poison, the bite would be a minor irritation, at best[31]. So, ladybugs, as far as I'm concerned, are not as lovable as we, or at least I, once thought.

Why am I talking about ladybugs when this book is about ghosts and hauntings? Because this next case involves a two-and-a-half-year-old girl, who we will call Samantha[*], who is afraid to be in her

---

[*] Name changed

bedroom because of the "lady" who lives in her room with her. She calls this frightening lady the "Ladybug." The Ladybug hides in her bedroom and continuously jumps out of her hiding place to frighten Samantha. Sounds pretty creepy and scary…doesn't it? I have conducted numerous investigations where young children were involved and some of the things they say are pretty amazing and sometimes downright frightening. Take the three-year-old daughter in one case I investigated in 2008. Amanda[*] and her mother Lisa were the only ones in the house at the time. Amanda was sitting on the stairs near the kitchen while her mother was making dinner. Amanda started singing and saying, "Lisa-Bisa, Lisa-Bisa" over and over. Lisa was shocked at what she was saying because this was the pet name her deceased grandfather used to call her. Lisa relayed that no one had called her that name since his passing some 19 years earlier. She asked Amanda where she learned that and Amanda pointed to a corner in the living room and said, "From that man." Lisa asked what man and Amanda pointed to the corner again and then lifted her arms in the air and said, "Oh, he's gone."

Another case involved a three-and-a-half-year-old boy who started having nightmares involving a black and white "car" that kept "tipping" over his bed while he was sleeping. I first thought he could be describing a police car, but he said there were no lights on the roof. A short time after the nightmares began, his mother was reading a book to him in his bedroom when she realized he wasn't paying attention to her. Instead, his eyes were following something throughout the bedroom, so she asked him what he was looking at. He replied he was looking at the policeman that "flipped" his bedroom over. When she asked her son to describe the policeman, he said he was wearing black shoes, a blue shirt and pants that he

---

[*] Name changed

described as the color of "nighttime" blue. He couldn't see the policeman's hair because he was wearing a hat. The boy's eyes then followed the policeman as he exited the room. When his mom asked if the policeman was still in the bedroom, the boy replied no and said, "He just went in the ambulance."

Another case involved a three-year-old boy. This is the story his mother relayed to me.

My husband and I own a restaurant, and I stopped at the restaurant to do a last-minute chore while I was out running errands. I was inside for 10 minutes or so, with my mom and my son, Michael* waiting in the car.

When I came out and got in the car my mom very adamantly and sternly said, 'Listen to what Michael's telling you before you move the car.'

We were parked facing the rear entrance of the restaurant, our 'employee' entrance, if you will, so I started to listen to my son. He began telling me a story about a 'string guy' and I'm listening and he's talking about the guy hanging from the rope by the restaurant ...our son is three years old.

He is a good boy, with no influences of what that kind of image would look like, nor has he ever spoken like this before. He's not imaginative in the regard of making up stuff, and if he does, it's about puppy dogs and kitty cats or blasting off to Mars, not a guy hanging from a rope.

So, he continues to talk and he's pointing to the area at the side of the building. So, I ask him questions like, 'What's the rope attached to?' ...he replies 'the metal thingy.' I ask him if I can take him out of the car so he can show me better about what he's talking about. He says 'no, if you get too close it will vanish.' I ask him, 'what does

69

that mean to you?' He says, vanish means 'if you get too close, it will disappear.' We went on like this for about 10 minutes and then he said, 'I just want to go home now, let's leave.' So, we leave, and the whole time I'm thinking maybe I'm overreacting, so we pull back and I ask my mom if we're on the same page and she's like yes, I wanted you to hear that because it was freaking me out. We pull out of the parking lot, and now that I don't think I'm completely crazy, I pull to the stop sign and I ask Michael 'what was the other end of the rope attached to' and he replies 'His neck.'

You can't make this stuff up, unless of course you're Stephen King.

Where do these young children get these seemingly bizarre and wild stories? Either they have fantastic imaginations at a young age or what they are describing and saying is real. Could it be that innocent children, who have not had enough life experiences, are unknowingly open to the world of the paranormal? Does a child's mind close down as they get older because adults tell them that ghosts are not real and they shouldn't have imaginary playmates?

There are several commonly held theories why young children can see and hear things others cannot. The first is that children's brains are proportionately larger than adult brains, approximately 135% larger, therefore they have more vivid imaginations and extended brain functions. A second theory is the brainwave connection. Young children are ruled by their own perception of life, for the most part. They have the power to talk to their imaginary friends, enjoying the world through unfiltered eyes and ideas of the world around them[32]. Another theory that is quite convincing is how humans see ultraviolet light, also known as UV light. Adults can only see between 400 and 700 nanometers above the electromagnetic spectrum. UV light falls just below the visible light at 315 and 400 nanometers. Infrared light falls above at 710 nanometers to 1 millimeter. Young children are able to see things around 380 nanometers, which places them in the UV range, meaning if ghosts "hang out" in the UV range like many paranormal experts believe, then children are seeing things that adults cannot[33]. Between the ages of 11 and 14, parts of the mind shut down as friends, parents, teachers and family tell them what is right and wrong and what is real and what is not[34].

Did or does your child have an imaginary playmate that he or she talks to and plays with? Did you have an imaginary playmate when you were a child? Was the playmate real to you? Maybe they are not imaginary at all -- maybe they are real. The next time your child mentions their imaginary playmate, pay close attention to what they are saying and ask questions. You may be in for a shock.

Back to the case of the Ladybug. We were first contacted in January 2010 by a family afraid of living in their home and desperately looking for answers to the scary and frightening things they were experiencing. The Medina County, Ohio, home was a small 918-square-foot, two-story, two-bedroom duplex with a kitchen, dining room and living room on the first floor and two bedrooms and a bathroom on the second floor. There was also a basement and attached one-car garage. Due to the confidentiality of our clients, I cannot disclose the city where this case took place. Confidentiality of our clients is of the utmost importance.

The family consisted of parents, Sharon and Mark[*] and their two-and-a-half-year-old daughter, Samantha. They moved into the duplex in the summer of 2007 when Samantha was just a baby. Everything was fine in the home until December of that year when things started happening inside their home that they couldn't

---

[*] Names changed

71

explain, such as phantom footsteps on the second floor and knockings coming from inside the walls of the second-floor master bedroom. It seemed that the majority of the activity would intensify in December and then gradually subside over the next several months. Along with the knockings in the master bedroom, other frightening occurrences started happening. One time, Mark was sleeping in his bed in the bedroom when he heard the sliding closet door slam open. Another time, he was lying in bed when something lifted his leg into the air and dropped it back down onto the bed!

Cold spots were constantly felt in the home, even though the thermostat was kept at 76 degrees.

One evening, Sharon and Mark were watching television in the living room when they noticed the door to the basement slowly opening on its own. Their hearts started racing as they expected to see something coming out of the basement, but there was nothing.

Sharon was also having physical problems while in the home and started feeling ill and cold all the time. She felt like there was a negative energy in the home.

Most of the more frightening incidents centered around Samantha, though. She started to refuse to sleep in her own bedroom at night because of the Ladybug jumping out and scaring her. She had no problem sleeping in the master bedroom by herself but was terrified to sleep in her own room. Strange things also started to happen to the small television set in her bedroom. One evening, Mark unplugged the television because it kept turning on by itself. Later, when he checked on the television, he discovered that it was plugged in again. Mark stated it was impossible for Samantha to get behind the dresser to plug the television in.

Samantha regularly had conversations with someone or something on the second floor, whom Sharon and Mark could not see or hear. One evening, Samantha was walking up the stairs to the second floor talking, when she stopped, screamed, turned around and ran down the stairs crying, saying "it" hurt her fingers. According to Sharon and Mark, when they looked at Samantha's fingers, they discovered her ring and pinky fingers were "beet" red! That was the last straw! They couldn't risk anymore harm to their daughter and reached out to us to see if we could help them.

We arrived at the home on January 23, 2010. Along with myself were my wife Kathy, daughter Amy and another investigator, Jake. We were given a tour of the home and once we got to Samantha's bedroom, almost all of us had very strong feelings that we described as suffocating and nauseating. During the tour, Mark told us he had been told by his neighbors that there was a death in his half of the duplex prior to them moving in, which was possibly due to a drug overdose.

During this investigation, we used a wide variety of equipment, including four stationary video cameras placed throughout the home, as well as two DVR infrared cameras. We also placed five audio recorders strategically throughout the home, concentrating on the master bedroom and Samantha's bedroom.

We split up into two teams of two investigators each. One team would investigate the two bedrooms on the second floor, while the other team watched the DVR monitor that was set up in the basement. Jake and Amy began the investigation on the second floor while Kathy, Sharon, Mark and myself stayed in the basement. Samantha was not present during the investigation. While investigating Samantha's bedroom, Jake heard strange noises coming from Samantha's bed, which sounded to him like the covers and blankets being moved. However, he did not actually see the covers moving. An hour later, the teams switched with Kathy and myself now investigating the second floor. Again, strange and unexplained noises, including tapping and rapping sounds, were heard coming from within Samantha's bedroom. We searched, but could not find the source of the strange noises. During the next portion of the investigation was when things turned crazy and scary, especially for Amy. Kathy and Amy went into Samantha's bedroom to continue the investigation. Jake and myself, along with Sharon and Mark, stayed in the basement watching the DVR monitor. During the equipment setup, we placed one of the DVR cameras in Samantha's room so the investigators in the basement could view what was going on in that room through the monitor. Amy was sitting on Samantha's bed and Kathy was sitting on the floor against the wall directly across from her. The rest of us were sitting around in the basement talking and watching the monitor when all of a sudden, the whole home shook and it sounded like there was an explosion! It was so loud, dust from the basement ductwork fell to the basement floor. My first thought was an airplane or large truck had struck the duplex. At the same time the "explosion" happened, we noticed on the monitor that Amy sprang from the bed as fast as she could. Kathy then radioed us on the walkie-talkie that we needed to get up to Samantha's bedroom, so all of us ran up the two flights of stairs from the basement into the bedroom. Amy appeared shaken and was breathing heavily when we entered the room. We asked Amy what happened and she relayed that Kathy and she were in the bedroom doing an EVP session. Kathy was sitting on the floor listening in real time to her audio recorder through the use of headphones. Amy said she was sitting on Samantha's bed when she started to feel the covers underneath her moving like they were being pulled. The bed then gently lifted off the floor and slammed back down. It scared the crap out of her and she couldn't get off the bed quickly enough! Once off the bed, she immediately turned her flashlight on and told Kathy what happened. Because it was so dark in the room, Kathy did not see what happened, but she obviously heard and felt it. Kathy said it was so loud in her headphones that it sounded like an atomic bomb!

We examined the bed, but could find no logical explanation as to what caused the bed to raise up and slam back down. During the investigation, all of us had sat on the bed at one time or another with no issues at all. Prior to the incident, Kathy stated, "I brought back Amy with me this time." Was this the Ladybug's way to welcome Amy into the "her" bedroom?

After several more hours of investigating, we packed up our equipment and left for the night. We reviewed all of the audio and video, but nothing else was discovered that could be considered paranormal.

The next day I received a phone call from Mark who told me that last night after we left, Sharon was sitting on the sofa in the living room when a can of pop on the coffee table crushed down as if something had sat on it. Sharon then felt something sit on the sofa beside her, at which time she became sick to her stomach. Mark also mailed me a copy of a police report he obtained referencing the death that occurred in his half of the duplex. According to the police report, a 41-year-old female named Pamela[*] was found deceased in her upstairs bedroom on December 26, several years prior to Mark's family moving in. As mentioned earlier by Mark and Sharon, most of the activity occurs in December. The police report went on to say that Pamela was a heavy drinker and was an abuser of illegal drugs.

---

[*] Name changed

The cause of death was listed as acute pancreatitis (days old) and chronic pancreatitis, caused by the long-term use of alcohol. Apparently, Pamela had been dead for several days before anyone found her.

Several symptoms of pancreatitis include nausea, irritability and feeling lightheaded. These symptoms correspond to what others have experienced in the home, especially Sharon, who was always feeling sick and nauseous.

Mark contacted me a few days later and stated he was sitting in the living room when he heard Samantha upstairs having a conversation with someone. He and Samantha were the only ones' home at the time. Mark became angry and ran upstairs, yelling at "it" to leave Samantha alone and to get out of his house. Mark then took Samantha downstairs to the living room, at which time Samantha said, "Pamela went bye-bye." Mark said the hair on the back of his neck stood up and he became frozen with fear. There was no way for Samantha to know that Pamela was the person who died in the duplex.

We returned to the home two weeks later on February 6th to conduct a follow-up investigation. Only three investigators made this investigation: Kathy, another investigator and myself. The only unusual thing to happen during this investigation involved walkie-talkies. Kathy and the other investigator were in Samantha's bedroom when a young child's voice came over the walkie-talkie saying, "Help me now." The child repeated "help me" several times within a three-minute time frame. The investigators kept asking who they were and what type of help they needed. The child never responded to their questions and it sounded like the child was trying to talk with someone else. We all know voices over a walkie-talkie don't seem very impressive or conclusive of any paranormal activity, but there were some things that we noticed that made it strange, anyway. The voice seemed distant, with a tinny echo. The child never responded to the investigators' questions. It seemed peculiar that the child was asking for help over a walkie-talkie. I was in the basement with Mark and Sharon and we never heard the child's voice come over our walkie-talkie. We did hear Kathy and the other investigator talking through it, though. As soon as Mark and I entered Samantha's bedroom, the strange voice stopped and did not return for the rest of the investigation.

We had no other personal experiences that night, however, after reviewing a video camera that was set up in the master bedroom, we did capture knockings that seemed to be coming from inside the bedroom. These knockings confirm what Sharon and Mark said was occurring there.

Here was a family who lived in fear, especially around Christmas time when the activity increased. Could the Ladybug have been Pamela, the previous tenant who died in the duplex? Was the Ladybug evil or negative, or was she just trying to contact the family, especially Samantha? I was aware that Mark called in other investigators to see what they could find. I have lost touch with Mark and his family, but I do hope they are not living in fear anymore and that the Ladybug was finally able to "fly off" to a better place.

Chapter Seven

GREAT BRITAIN

GHOSTS ACROSS THE ATLANTIC

Imagine living in Great Britain in the 17th century, the "Age of Reason" or even in an earlier time? What would it be like? Today, we take everything for granted from modern day bathrooms and toilet paper to the internet. What about turning on a light when you walk into a room or getting hungry while watching your favorite evening television show and going into your refrigerator to get a bite to eat? What about vacations? Did they have tourist spots back then? If so, how long would it take to get to their destination? What about illness? What would that be like a thousand years ago? Nowadays we take over-the-counter and prescription medicine that can ease or take care of our symptoms. How long would their symptoms last without any medication, urgent care centers, emergency rooms or hospitals? How would they feel? Here is one reason I am thankful I did not live back then…a medical emergency. What if you broke your leg, had a bowel obstruction, severe lacerations or any other type of injury or serious physical ailment? How long would you have to wait for any type of help or anything to ease the pain…hours, days, for the rest of your life? Could this be a reason that so many old and historic places around the world are haunted due to all the pain, suffering, famine, war and atrocities that have occurred in the past?

Great Britain, which includes England, Scotland and Wales, is a country filled with haunted homes, inns, cemeteries and castles, and is home to some of the most haunted places in the world. Great Britain should be on every paranormal investigator and enthusiast's bucket list. If you checked to see where some of the most haunted places in the world are, these seven locations invariably show up on many of the lists: Ancient Ram Inn, Tower of London, Raynham Hall, Highgate Cemetery and Berry Pomeroy Castle all in England, plus Edinburgh Castle and Edinburgh Vaults in Edinburgh, Scotland. In fact, some people consider Edinburgh to be one of the most haunted cities in the world.

Ever since I can remember, there were two places in the world that I wanted to visit more than any other, Loch Ness and the Tower of London. The first things that comes to mind when these two locations are mentioned are prehistoric monsters and executions. Another location I wanted to visit and spend the night was a haunted castle and there are plenty of haunted castle hotels in Great Britain, including Lumley, Thornbury, Walworth and Chillingham castles in England and Tulloch, Culzean and Dalhousie castles in Scotland.

In 2010, my wife Kathy and I decided it was time to vacation in Great Britain. This was a dream come true for me and a trip of a lifetime.

LONDON

On September 25, 2010, Kathy and I flew from Dulles Airport in Washington, DC, to London Heathrow Airport. Flying to Europe is an awesome experience with several serious drawbacks. The first is the time change, with London being five hours ahead of the United States Eastern Standard Time Zone. When it is noon in Washington, DC, it is 5:00 PM in London. We departed Dulles at 6:40 PM and arrived in London around 7:05 AM on Sunday, the 26th. This wasn't too bad for us since we were booked in upper class on Virgin Atlantic. Upper class is a step above first class as each passenger in upper class has their own private area, complete with television, footstool, champagne, breakfast and turn-down service where they make your seat and stool into a bed, complete with sheets, blankets and a pillow. Checking into your hotel is another drawback, unless you make prior arrangements with your hotel, which we unfortunately did not. We arrived at our hotel around 9:00 AM, but our check-in wasn't until 3:00 PM. This, along with jet lag, was going to make for a very long and tiring first day! Luckily, the hotel held our luggage so we didn't have to lug it all over London. We were spending two weeks in England and Scotland and had a ton of luggage. Since our hotel was right along the Thames, we decided to walk along the river seeing whatever we could. The first place we headed was, of course, the Tower of London, only about 1 ¾ miles from our hotel. We arrived just as it was opening.

Tower of London

The Tower of London[35], founded in 1066, is a castle fortress on the north bank of the Thames and is officially known as Her Majesty's Royal Palace and Fortress of the Tower of London. The most recognizable part of the fortress and where the Tower of London gets its name is the White Tower, which was built in 1078 by William the Conqueror. The Tower of London consists of the White Tower in the center of the fortress, with numerous buildings surrounding it. Encompassing this complex of buildings is an inner wall with strategically placed towers and an outer wall with similar towers. There is a total of 21 towers that comprise the Tower of London, with the whole fortress then surrounded by a moat. The Tower of London was used as a prison from 1100 until 1952, but that was not its original function. Early on it served as a royal residence.

When most people hear of the Tower of London, they think torture, death, executions and beheadings, but the fact is only seven people were executed, beheaded to be exact, within the walls prior to the 20th century in an area called Tower Green[36]. Those seven individuals executed on Tower Green were William Hastings in 1483, Queen Anne Boleyn on May 19, 1536, Margaret Pole, Countess of Salisbury on May 27, 1541, Queen Catherine Howard on February 13, 1542, Jane Boleyn on February 13, 1542, Lady Jane Grey on February 12, 1554 and Robert Devereux on February 25, 1601. In addition, three more people were executed within the fortress by firing squad on July 19, 1743. However, numerous individuals who were held prisoner in the tower later met their fate at Tower Hill, just north of the Tower of London, where some 112 executions took place with the majority of those also beheadings.

Another little-known fact about the Tower of London concerns torture. Although it did happen, it wasn't as common as most people believe. Torture was only used in the 16th and 17th centuries on a small portion of the prisoners. Even then, there were only three main types of torture devices used: the rack, the Scavenger's Daughter and the manacles[37]. Prisoners were placed on the rack lying on their back, with their arms stretched out over their heads. Their hands and feet were bound to the rack, which was slowly turned, stretching the hapless victim until their limbs were dislocated and ripped from their sockets. The Scavenger's Daughter was a torture device that, instead of stretching the body, slowly compresses the victim's body. The victim was placed in the device in a crouched-kneeling position. As the device was tightened, it slowly brought the victim's face to their knees until blood started flowing out of their ears and nose. The last torture device, which was more commonly used, was the manacles, a simple torture device in which iron manacles (handcuffs) were secured around the victims' wrists. The victim would then be lifted off the ground with their wrists holding the weight of their body.

As you can see, even though executions and torture within the Tower of London was not common, it did happen. The extreme emotion, suffering and fears that prisoners felt created the perfect formula for a haunting. Add the fact that the Tower of London was also a prison, and you have the workings of an extremely haunted location.

There are numerous ghosts that have been seen and reported over the years inside the tower. Witnesses have seen the ghosts of Anne Boleyn, King Henry VI, Lady Jane Grey, Margaret Pole, Lady Arbella Stuart and even a bear inside the Tower of London. The headless ghost of Anne Boleyn[38], which is the most prevalent, has been seen wandering the area of Tower Green holding her head under her arm. She has also been seen walking around the White Tower, as well as in the Chapel Royal of St. Peter ad Vincula inside the tower. Another ghost story involves a guard who was protecting the Crown Jewels outside Martin Tower where the jewels use to be held, when an apparition of a large bear started to approach him. It is said the guard died two days later, apparently of fright. It is interesting to note that at one time, the Tower of London used to hold a menagerie of wild animals, including bears[39].

We did not visit the Tower of London as investigators, but as tourists. However, both my wife and I did have an unusual experience in one of the inner wall towers, the Salt Tower (photo 24). The Salt Tower is located in the southeast corner of the fortress and consists of a dungeon basement, ground floor and second floor.

It was on the second floor where my wife and I had our experience. Once inside the tower, my wife and I went our separate ways exploring the modestly small room. On the walls were graffiti that was carved by victims who were imprisoned inside the room. While walking around the room, I started to feel dizzy and my equilibrium began to falter. It felt like I was trying to walk on a small boat on the ocean that was rolling from side to side. I had never felt like this before and I had to get out of there before I became sick. I made my

Photo 24 - Kathy inside the Salt Tower

way to the door and, once I exited the room, the feeling went away and I immediately felt better. My wife exited the room shortly after saying that she had to get out of that room because she started to feel dizzy and sick! Unbeknownst to each other, we both suffered the same physical experience. In later research, I discovered that the Salt Tower was used as a prison and is considered one of the most haunted locations inside the Tower of London, which we did not know at the time. One of the prisoners who was held in the room was a Jesuit priest named Henry Walpole[40]. Walpole was repeatedly tortured on the rack, but even throughout all his suffering, he never confessed to any crimes. He was eventually transferred to York, where he was executed by being hanged, drawn and quartered on April 7, 1595. No wonder we felt the way we did. There seems to be a lot of emotional energy left over from when the Salt Tower was used as a prison and torture chamber.

After we left the Tower of London, we crossed the Tower Bridge to the south bank of the Thames where we entered the London Bridge Experience[41]. Guests are led by actors on a tour through the "dark" moments of London's history, which included battles with the Romans, The Great Fire of London and a medieval encounter with Vikings. History of all the London Bridges that have been on the site are also explained. It should be noted that there have been several bridges called London Bridge. The "New" London Bridge, which was in use from 1831 to 1967, was dismantled stone by stone and rebuilt in Lake Havasu City, Arizona with a rededication ceremony in 1971. We then crossed over the current London Bridge to the north side and finally were able to check in to our hotel. After a long day of sightseeing, it was nice to finally get some rest.

We only spent a couple more days in London and visited a few historical places, including Westminster Abbey, Banqueting Hall, the National Gallery and Buckingham Palace for the changing of the guards. The only other "paranormal" excursions we did was a ghost walk and a Jack the Ripper walking tour. The ghost walk wasn't really a ghost walk, but mostly a history walking tour with a couple of ghost stories thrown in here and there. The Jack the Ripper walking tour was cool if you're into that sort of thing, which I am. I am interested in the unknown and mysteries, including the case of Jack the Ripper, one of the greatest unsolved murder mysteries of all time. The tour took visitors through the dark, foggy streets and back alleys in the Whitechapel District, where in 1888, Jack the Ripper prowled looking for his victims.

On Wednesday, September 29, we left the City of London and headed north on the East Coast Main Line train for the 4 ½ hour, 400-mile trip to Edinburgh, Scotland.

Tower of London
London, EC3N 4AB
Phone: +44 (0)20 3166 6000
Website: www.hrp.org.uk/tower-of-london

London
Website: www.visitlondon.com.

EDINBURGH

Alec, a friend of ours, was waiting at the train station when we arrived in Edinburgh, pronounced Ed-in-buh-ruh and not Ed-in-burg. When we got to his car, I started to worry because his car was so small, I could put my hand on top of the roof and roll it back in forth! How were we going to fit six pieces of luggage and three adults into this tiny vehicle? Alec said, "Don't worry, everything is under control" and proceeded to put ALL the luggage inside the vehicle like he was casually putting a puzzle together. I don't know how he did it, but he did. We crammed into his car and Alec drove us to his home in Penicuik, just outside of Edinburgh, where we stayed several nights with him and his wife Janice.

Edinburgh Castle

On Thursday, September 30, Kathy and I took the bus into Edinburgh to do some sightseeing. We especially wanted to walk the Royal Mile[42] and visit Edinburgh Castle[43]. Historically, the Royal Mile was the main road between Edinburgh Castle and Holyrood Palace, the official residence of the British Monarch of Scotland. Today, it is the main tourist destination in Edinburgh with its eclectic mix of restaurants, shops, pubs and attractions. Once we were dropped off, we made our way to Edinburgh Castle by walking the Royal Mile, stopping along the way to visit shops and attractions. The castle sits atop Castle Rock, which is actually an extinct volcano at the western end of the Royal Mile. The oldest part of the castle dates to the 12th century and has been the scene of many battles and conflicts. Research undertaken in 2014 identified 26 sieges in its 1,100-year history, giving it the claim to having been "the most besieged place in Great Britain and one of the most attacked locations in the world." No wonder it is considered one of the most haunted places in Great Britain, and just like other castle fortresses, it had its fair share of dungeons, torture and executions. There have been numerous reports of paranormal activity from both visitors and employees alike. Two of the more popular hauntings are that of a headless drummer[44] and the sound of his drumming along the battlements, as well as the sightings of Lady Jane Douglas of Glamis[45]. Lady Jane was imprisoned in the castle dungeon after she was accused of being a witch. She was burned at the stake on July 17, 1537, after her servants and family were tortured into admitting her guilt. Kathy and I did enjoy the day touring Edinburgh Castle and learning of its history, however, we did not encounter any paranormal activity.

Edinburgh Castle
Edinburgh Castle
Castlehill
Edinburgh
EH1 2NG
Phone: +44 (0)131 225 9846
Website: www.edinburghcastle.scot

Penicuik House

That evening, Alec and Janice took us to a lesser known haunted location in their hometown of Penicuik, aptly called Penicuik House. We had never heard of Penicuik House before, but both Kathy and I were excited to go. We piled into Alec's car and off we went. After several minutes driving some dark, lonely roads, Alec pulled off into a small parking lot. We got out of the car and walked down a well-maintained asphalt path through the dark woods. It was a cool, clear night with the stars shining brightly. We walked about a half mile when the woods opened up into a large field and there it was silhouetted against the night sky, a grand shell of a small castle estate -- Penicuik House.

Penicuik House[46] was built in 1761 by Sir James Clerk, the 4th Laird of Penicuik and 3rd Baronet. (In Scotland, a Laird is the owner of a large estate. A Baronet is a member of the lowest hereditary titled British order with the status of a commoner, but able to use the prefix "Sir.") In 1899, the estate was gutted by a fire and left abandoned, a shell of its former grandeur.

Alec and Janice relayed that the site is allegedly haunted by a Lady in White who has been seen wandering the estate. It is said she was one of the last Lady Clerks to reside in the estate prior to the devastating fire.

Restoration work was in progress, as there was scaffolding and fencing around the structure. I expressed my concerns about trespassing on the property, but Alec said the owners don't mind as long as we don't go inside. Alec would know since he is a retired Edinburgh police officer. We would not have gone inside the building anyway due to safety concerns. The structure was massive with the length approximately 220' long and the width about 95' wide, making the first floor alone a staggering 20,900 square feet! We roamed around the massive structure, taking photographs, conducting EVP recordings and checking for EMF and temperature readings. The temperature was about 54 degrees and there were

some minor EMF spikes near the northwest end of the structure. Later during our investigation, I captured a strange mist in a photograph enveloping Janice and Kathy (photo 25). About that same time, Janice jumped, let out a little scream and said something just grabbed her

Photo 25 – Janice, Kathy and strange mist

"bum!" There was no one standing behind Janice, at least that was visible to us. It really startled Janice, as this was her first paranormal experience. It is always enjoyable to see other people have paranormal experiences, especially if they never had one before. We investigated a little longer, but since we had no other experiences, we decided to leave.

The restoration project at Penicuik House is ongoing. Here is their vision statement:[47]

"Our vision is to secure an exciting and sustainable future for Penicuik House and Designed Landscape, making it an appealing, accessible and inspiring place for new and existing audiences to visit, support and enjoy – now and for years to come."

Penicuik House
Find Penicuik House:
EH26 9LA
Phone: 01968 670738
Website: www.penicuikhouse.co.uk/

Rosslyn Chapel

Photo 26 - Kathy at Rosslyn Chapel

They next day, we drove to Roslin, Scotland, home of the famous Rosslyn Chapel (photo 26). Many of you may remember the Rosslyn Chapel from the 2006 movie *The Da Vinci Code,* starring Tom Hanks where actual scenes from the movie were filmed. The Rosslyn Chapel[48] dates from the mid-15th century and has accumulated its share of ghost stories in its 500-plus-year history. It is said that visitors have encountered spirits that vanish before their eyes. There are also reports of a black knight on horseback that has been seen around the chapel and a lady in white, which seems every historical building in Great Britain has[49]. It is believed that a knight by the name of Sir William Sinclair who died in battle is buried beneath the chapel in full armor.

The architecture outside and inside the chapel is beautifully elaborate. I have never seen anything like this before in my life. It seemed every inch inside the chapel was intricately carved with figures and scenes, such as knights on horseback, angels, the dance of death and even carvings of Lucifer, but the most unusual and mysterious carvings are those that appear to be ears of corn. Ears of corn carved into a structure that was built in 1446, almost 50 years before Columbus discovered North America? Corn or maize, as it is known, was first cultivated some 10,000 years ago by the indigenous peoples of Mexico. Corn was not introduced into Europe until after the arrival of Europeans in 1492, so how can there be images of corn carved inside Rosslyn Chapel?[50] Another one of history's mysteries.

Again, we did not come to investigate -- that would have been difficult with the number of tourists there and the fact they do not allow paranormal investigations. In fact, photography inside the chapel was strictly forbidden, but it didn't matter to us. Rosslyn Chapel was one of the most mysterious and beautiful buildings we have ever seen.

Today, Rosslyn Chapel is a working church part of the Scottish Episcopal Church in the Diocese of Edinburgh. Visitors are welcome to attend any of the services.

Photo 27 - Rosslyn Chapel

Rosslyn Chapel
Rosslyn Chapel, Chapel Loan
Roslin, Midlothian, EH25 9PU
Phone: 0131 440 2159
Website: www.rosslynchapel.com
Note: Rosslyn Chapel Trust does not permit paranormal investigations.

Greyfriars Kirkyard/Covenanters' Prison/MacKenzie Poltergeist

Later that day, Kathy and I ventured to Greyfriars Kirkyard[51], a cemetery dating from 1561 that surrounds Greyfriars Kirk in Edinburgh. Kirk is a Scottish word meaning church. Greyfriars Kirkyard is home to many notable people throughout Scotland's history and is considered one of the most haunted cemeteries in the world. It is also home to two of the most terrifying locations in Edinburgh: Covenanters' Prison[52] and the Black Mausoleum, home to the MacKenzie Poltergeist[53]. The MacKenzie Poltergeist is one of the most documented and terrifying poltergeists of all time. Since 1998, more than 500 visitors to Greyfriars Kirkyard and Covenanters' Prison, in particular, have been psychically attacked by an unseen force. Visitors have been pushed, scratched and have had their hair pulled, resulting in bruises, scratches and even broken bones. Others have passed out or vomited. The attacks were so bad and numerous that Covenanters' Prison was locked off from the rest of the cemetery. Who or what was the MacKenzie Poltergeist and what is Covenanters' Prison and the Black Mausoleum?

On February 28, 1638, numerous Scotsmen signed the National Covenant[54], an agreement born in Greyfriars Kirkyard in which Scotland would defend Presbyterianism against the desire of King Charles I who wanted Scotland to follow the religion of England. Scotland wanted the freedom to practice whichever religion they desired, but they would also remain loyal to the king. In 1677, Sir George MacKenzie[55] was appointed Lord Advocate of Scotland by King Charles II. MacKenzie was a 17th century judge and Lord Advocate and was known as "Bluidy (Bloody) MacKenzie." A Lord Advocate is the chief legal officer for the Scottish government in both criminal and civil matters. King Charles II demanded that

Scotland follow the religion of England and to renounce their Presbyterian religion, which they refused. Religious differences were a cause for many persecutions, conflicts and wars in world history and Scotland in the 17th century was no different.

On June 22, 1679, Presbyterian Covenanters were defeated at the Battle of Bothwell Bridge[56] near Bothwell, South Lanarkshire, Scotland, by royalist troops. It was an overwhelming defeat for the Covenanters, with about 3,000 taken prisoner to Greyfriars Kirkyard where some of them, on orders from MacKenzie, were tortured, hanged and beheaded for their part in the uprising and their religious beliefs. Others were transferred to other prisons or released. Approximately 1,200 of the surviving Covenanter prisoners were moved to a small open-air prison adjacent to Greyfriars. The majority of these prisoners died from starvation, disease and

Photo 28 - Tomb of George MacKenzie

exposure, with many of the bodies buried inside Greyfriars. In all, MacKenzie was responsible for more than 18,000 deaths, most of them his own countrymen. The time of MacKenzie's persecution of the Covenanters was known as "The Killing Time." It is ironic that when MacKenzie died in 1691, he was buried in Greyfriars (photo 28), very near to what became known as Covenanters' Prison and near his former countrymen, many of whom he persecuted. It is in this portion of Greyfriars Kirkyard where the majority of the poltergeist attacks have taken place.

In 1998, a vagrant broke into the MacKenzie tomb, defiling and vandalizing it. He even tried breaking into the casket containing the body of Sir George MacKenzie. It is after this break-in that the MacKenzie Poltergeist came to be. Was the malevolent spirit of Sir George MacKenzie awakened or was it something else? Many people believe it is the ghost of MacKenzie that has returned, but could it also be the Covenanters buried in the cemetery who awoke to protect themselves from MacKenzie and anyone who ventured into Covenanters' Prison? It would be very interesting to know the religious beliefs of those attacked by the poltergeist.

Today Covenanters' Prison (photo 29) is located at the southwest corner of Greyfriars Kirkyard and is surrounded by a high stone wall. The "prison" itself is lined with old mausoleums and is cut off from the rest of the cemetery by a locked gate. Inside Covenanters'

Photo 29 - Covenanter's Prison

Prison is a tomb known as the Black Mausoleum, which was the focal point of the majority of the poltergeist attacks. The gates to the prison are only opened during a ghost walk, which of course we went on. Note: MacKenzie's tomb is also known as the Black Mausoleum.

Just like other haunted walking tours we have taken, this one took us to some of the most haunted locations Edinburgh has to offer. The tour was pretty good with a fun and knowledgeable guide (most of the time it is the guide that can make or break a tour), but the best part of the tour was when we were taken inside Covenanters' Prison and the Black Mausoleum. The group, including our friends Alec and Janice, crammed our way inside the Black Mausoleum. There, our guide told us about the horrific stories surrounding Covenanters' Prison and the MacKenzie Poltergeist. The guide believed that the entity feeds off the energy that, we as human beings, emit. At the end of the tour, everyone was escorted out of the prison and the gates were locked. Kathy and I, along with Alec and Janice, stayed to talk with our guide further. We told our guide that we were paranormal investigators from the United States. After chatting for a while, the guide, along with other members of the tour company, decided to unlock the gates and let us back inside to investigate Covenanters' Prison and the Black Mausoleum. Wow, what a great opportunity! It also didn't hurt that Alec was a retired Edinburgh Police Officer who used to do foot patrol on the Royal Mile. The gate was unlocked and all of us walked back to the Black Mausoleum (photo 30 and

Photo 30 - Kathy inside the Black Mausoleum

31) where we went inside the shadowy and frightful tomb where numerous visitors have been attacked. This time, it would just be Kathy, Janice, Alec and I alone inside the mausoleum armed with a digital audio recorder, EMF and temperature meters, and a

digital camera. We started off our investigation with an EVP session when, after a few minutes into the session, Kathy reported that something tugged on her pant leg. A couple minutes later, an EVP was captured on the audio recorder. We cannot understand what is being said, but it sounds like someone yelling. After we finished investigating the Black Mausoleum, we went to another mausoleum to continue the investigation, but nothing paranormal was captured

or felt. Unfortunately, we did not get to investigate much longer, but we didn't mind. We did capture one possible EVP and Kathy had physical contact. We were just very grateful that we were allowed and privileged to investigate this fantastic location.

Photo 31 - The Black Mausoleum

Greyfriars Kirkyard
26A Candlemaker Row
Edinburgh EH1 2QE, UK
Phone: +44 131 664 4314
Website: www.greyfriarskirk.com

Edinburgh Vaults

Later during our stay in Edinburgh, we took a ghost tour of the world-famous and extremely haunted Edinburgh Vaults[57]. The Edinburgh Vaults, completed in 1788, are a series of 120 underground chambers and rooms located beneath the South Bridge. South Bridge is a street bridge consisting of 19 arches, but currently only one of the arches is visible from the street as it crosses another street below. Today, South Bridge looks like your ordinary city street with sidewalks, buildings, shops, offices, restaurants and bars lining both sides of the street. You would never guess you were walking or driving on a bridge or that once there was a "living city" beneath you.

The vaults (photo 32) were originally built for storage, workshops and living space for the businesses above, but due to poor construction, the vaults started flooding some 30 years later and were eventually abandoned, but that doesn't mean they were

Photo 32 – A section of the Edinburgh Vaults

totally uninhabited. After the vaults were abandoned, the homeless started moving into the vaults. Along with the homeless came illicit pubs, brothels, gambling establishments and disease. Thieves, rapists and murderers prowled the subterranean complex with crimes running rampant since there were no laws or police patrolling the vaults. It was a lawless society and a horrific way to live with assaults, robberies, rapes and murders an everyday occurrence. Some legends say that serial killers stalked the vaults looking for victims whose bodies would be sold for medical research as Edinburgh was one of the most prominent cities for the research of anatomical study in the early part of the 19th century. As you can see again, here is a perfect formula for a prime haunted location.

No one knows when the vaults permanently closed. Some say it was in the 1820s; others say it was in the 1870s. Whatever date the Edinburgh Vaults were lost to time, they were not rediscovered until 1988. Since their rediscovery, there have been reports of paranormal

activity inside the dark and secluded rooms of the vaults. Visitors have experienced everything from cold spots and phantom voices to a child ghost who likes to hold visitors' hands. The most well-known of all of the activity in the vaults is a presence

Photo 33 -Kathy Investigating the Edinburgh Vaults

named "Mr. Boots." It is said Mr. Boots likes to hide in the dark recesses of the vaults throwing stones and rocks at unsuspecting visitors. Visitors have also heard his heavy footsteps walking through the passages of the vaults.

Kathy and I, plus Janice and Alec, took a ghost walking tour of the vaults. It was a day tour as we had no other evenings available to do a night tour. Our tour was a little over an hour and was very interesting and exciting at the same time. It didn't matter that the tour was during the day as there is no way to distinguish between day and night while inside the vaults, for they are in perpetual darkness. We were told tales of murder, torture, serial killers, ghosts and Mr. Boots. After the tour was over, we chatted with the tour guide and told her that Kathy and I were paranormal investigators from the United States. She agreed to take us back inside the vaults to conduct a little investigation. There again, it didn't hurt that Alec was a retired Edinburgh police officer who used to patrol this very same area on foot. We went back inside and walked around for a short time until we finally picked a room to conduct an EVP session. This room had a plastic skeleton shackled to a pillory (photo 34) with water seeping in from above. During this session, we captured two possible EVPs. The first one sounded like a male saying "No" and the second one sounded like a female saying "Flash," which doesn't make sense. During an investigation, whenever a photograph is being taken using a flash, the photographer usually says "flash" to warn others that there will be a flash so as not

Photo 34 – An unlucky victim

to blind them. There were five of us inside the vault: Kathy, Janice, Alec, our female tour guide and myself. I was the only one using a camera and didn't take a photograph at that time, nor did I say flash at that time. Our guide told us about some activity in another room where several visitors in the past couple of days had been touched on the back of the head. We proceeded to that room where we were allowed to investigate a little while longer. We weren't touched on the back of the head, nor did we have any other paranormal experiences, so we had to call it quits so the tour guide could prepare for the next tour. It was an exciting day in the Edinburgh Vaults and a bucket list experience, but we had one more stop to make just outside of Edinburgh...Dalhousie Castle.

Edinburgh Vaults
City of the Dead Tours
Greyfriars Funeral Bothy.
26A Candlemaker Row (just inside the graveyard entrance).
Edinburgh EH1 2QE
Phone: +44 131 225 9044 (abroad)
Phone: 0131 225 9044 (in the UK)
Website: www.cityofthedeadtours.com

Dalhousie Castle

Dalhousie Castle[58] (photo 35) is located near the town of Bonnyrigg, about 7 ½ miles southeast of Edinburgh Castle. The castle that originally stood on this spot was constructed in the 13th century by Symon de Ramesie (Simon of Ramsay) and was a stopping point for King Edward I on his way to defeat William Wallace at the Battle

of Falkirk in 1298 AD. You may remember William Wallace and Edward the Longshanks from the 1995 Academy Award-winning movie *Braveheart*. Simon of Ramsey is considered the founder of the Scottish Lowland Clan Ramsay, with the

Photo 35 - Dalhousie Castle

Ramsays of Dalhousie occupying lands in and around Dalhousie Castle. Changing hands several times between Scotland and England, the castle and neighboring countryside were the scenes of many battles and sieges throughout the wars for Scottish independence. In 1644, Oliver Cromwell stayed in Dalhousie Castle, using it as a base of operations for his invasion of Scotland.

Dalhousie Castle is currently a hotel spa[59] with 29 guest rooms, full-service spa (Aqueous Spa), two restaurants (Dungeon Restaurant and The Orangery) a bar (Library Bar), plus falconry and archery on the grounds. One of the more unusual features of the castle is the Dungeon Restaurant with its arched stone ceilings and suits of armor located in an area that was once used as the castle's dungeon. The original dungeon, which is still visible today, was where prisoners were lowered by rope into a hole in the ground, with no chance of escape. Some of the foundations and vaulted cellars date from the 13th century with the majority of the castle dating from the 15th century and on.

Dalhousie Castle has its share of ghosts. In fact, it has been considered one of the top 10 most haunted castles in the world, as well as one of the most haunted hotels in the world, ranking with famous haunted American hotels such as the Queen Mary,

Photo 36 - Kathy at Dalhousie Castle

Biltmore, Hotel Del Coronado and the Stanley. Dalhousie has three main ghosts that have been reported: Sir Alexander Ramsay, Lady Catherine Ramsay and Petra, a dog.

Sir Alexander Ramsay of Dalhousie[60], a Scottish patriot, was imprisoned in 1342 at Hermitage Castle near Newcastleton, Roxburghshire, Scotland, near the English border, where he died of starvation. He was actually imprisoned by a friend of his who was jealous that Ramsay was appointed sheriff instead of him. Even though Ramsay died at Hermitage Castle, some say his ghost haunts the halls of Dalhousie Castle. Another ghost that has been seen and heard is Petra[61], a dog that died in the 1980s when it fell to its death from one of the castle turrets, but the most prevalent ghost is that of Lady Catherine Ramsay[62]. There are a couple stories surrounding the death of 16-year-old Lady Catherine Ramsay. The first one tells how Lady Catherine was a mistress of one of the Ramsays. When his wife found out, she had Lady Catherine banished to a tower room where she was starved to death. Another story tells how Lady Catherine fell in love with a stable boy, but her parents would not allow her to see someone that low in society. Distraught over not being able to see the boy, Lady Catherine locked herself in a tower room where she starved herself to death…another love story gone bad. Either way, it appears Lady Catherine starved to death in one of the tower rooms. Lady Catherine, now known as the Lady in Gray because of the gray dress with puffy sleeves she has been seen in, is known to sit at the foot of guests' beds and has been seen wandering the staircases and the Dungeon Restaurant.

Kathy and I spent three nights at the castle in the William Wallace bedroom located on the top floor. Since there were no elevators inside the castle, we had to lug all of our luggage up the stairs, but we did have our own private battlement with breathtaking views of the surrounding countryside. Since this was a castle hotel spa, we spent one full day getting spa treatments. Both Kathy and I had five treatments each plus a spa lunch. Spa treatments in a luxurious haunted castle? We didn't have to die to go to Heaven -- we were already there! Such is the life of a paranormal investigator! We only spent one night investigating the castle, but it was a very worthwhile and productive investigation.

We heard the Dungeon Restaurant was one of the most active locations in the castle, so that is where we concentrated our efforts. Armed with a video camera, digital camera, audio recorder and EMF meter, we descended into the dark restaurant. The room was extremely dark as there are no windows and the little light there was came from a few electric candles on the walls. The restaurant was divided into three dining rooms, all of them containing tables with white tablecloths and elegant red high-backed chairs. The first room (photo 37) had numerous tables throughout. The second room (photo 38) was set up with one long table in the center. The third room (photo 39), located between the other two, was small with only four two-person tables. Candles, suits of armor, paintings and medieval weaponry, axes,

Photo 37 - The Dungeon Restaurant

swords, pikes and shields lined the stone walls. It was quiet except for some soft music that was piped in. We started off our investigation in the first dining room. I was responsible for the video recording, along with checking for EMF, while Kathy took photographs and audio recordings. We were sitting at tables at opposite sides of the room when Kathy heard a strange noise directly in front of her. Kathy couldn't see what made the noise as it was so dark in this room we could barely see each other. Kathy asked me if I made any type of noise, to which I responded, "No, I had not." She immediately started taking photographs directly across the table from where she was sitting. The first couple of photographs showed a dark-reddish blob in the upper left side of the photos that seemed to slowly move from the first to the second photograph. The

Photo 38 – The Dungeon Restaurant

blob was not visible in the photographs taken immediately after these two. Neither of us observed anything with our naked eyes. A little while later, we unintentionally scared the crap out of an employee of the hotel who was leaving for the night. Unfortunately, for this employee, he decided to leave through a dark, creepy restaurant with American tourists "hiding" in the darkness. He nearly jumped out of his pants when he came upon us. I don't think he was expecting that! I felt bad and said, "Didn't mean to scare ya!" We laughed it

Photo 39 – The Dungeon Restaurant

off and he left. Right as he left the restaurant, we captured an EVP of a male voice whispering, "Don't go." Was "someone" asking the employee not to leave him alone with these crazy Americans?!? Whatever the reason, it was a great piece of evidence and the sign of an intelligent haunting. We investigated the first dining room a little further and then went into the other two dining rooms, taking photographs, video and audio recordings. After a few more hours of investigating, we decided to call it a night. Later during the review of the audio recordings, we came upon something strange, something we had never captured on a recording before. In the first dining room, we captured what sounded like a dog walking across the floor. You could clearly hear the distinct sound of its nails clicking as it walked across the hard floor. Could this be the spirit of Petra, the dog who fell to its death some 20-plus years ago? I know spirits of animals can return, as mentioned in Chapter 4 with

Sneakers the cat, but this was the first time I caught possible evidence of an animal…how amazing!

We loved staying at and investigating Dalhousie Castle, but all good things must come to an end and we had to move on.

Dalhousie Castle Hotel
Edinburgh EH19 3JB, UK
Phone: +44 1875 820153
Website: www.dalhousiecastle.co.uk

Edinburgh
Marketing Edinburgh Ltd.
26 Frederick Street
Edinburgh
EH2 2JR
Phone: 0131 473 3666
Website: www.edinburgh.org

INVERNESS

On Saturday, October 2nd we woke up early to a bright, beautiful day. After breakfast, Alec drove us to Edinburgh Airport where we picked up a rental car, for today was the day when Kathy and I would be driving north to Inverness, Scotland, the gateway to Loch Ness. I was extremely excited and nervous about our little trip, as this is something I have wanted to do since childhood, but there was just one problem -- I had never driven on the left side of the road, let alone driven from the right side of a vehicle, and this would be more than a three-hour drive. Luckily, we paid a little more for an automatic, or not only would I have had to remember to stay in the proper lane, but I would also have had to shift gears using my left hand on the shifter. It was a good thing I could still use my right foot for the gas pedal, or who knows how this little expedition would have gone! It was also a good thing Kathy was with me. Her job as navigator was to make sure I stayed in the proper lane, especially when making any left or right-hand turns. I was white-knuckled in fear while driving out of the airport! I believe my fingers left imprints on the steering wheel…glad the car rental company didn't charge me extra for damaging their car! Thankfully it didn't take me too long to get accustomed to driving on the left side, and in no time, I felt like I had been driving in Scotland all my life. After making a couple stops along the way, including visiting our first distillery in Scotland, Dalwhinnie Distillery, we arrived at our home for the next few nights, Castle Stuart.

Castle Stuart

Castle Stuart[63], one of the top-rated castle hotels in all of Europe, according to traveler popularity, was completed in 1625 by James Stuart, 3rd Earl of Moray. The small, fairytale tower-house style castle has a dining room, drawing room, billiard room, kitchen and great hall, plus eight guest bedrooms. This was a perfect place for us to stay, as it is only about 11 ½ miles northeast from Loch Ness and only 3 miles north of the 1746 Battle of Culloden battlefield and need I say it…it is haunted.

We pulled up to the castle gate and after we confirmed who we were through the intercom system, the gate was opened. We drove down a tree-lined drive toward the castle and the parking lot where we were greeted outside by the owner and several Shetland ponies.

We were taken to our room, the Battlement Suite, or "MacLachlan" room as it is known, at the top of the west tower. Again, as there were no elevators inside the castle, we had a fun and difficult time lugging our suitcases up the circular tower staircase to our bedroom. While ascending the stairway, we had to be careful of the "tripping" steps. A "tripping" step[64] is a shorter step than all the rest, that was designed into medieval castles. Their purpose was to trip up and bog down attackers who were rushing up the stairs in battle, which would give the defenders coming down the stairs a tactical advantage.

Castle Stuart is one place we definitely wanted to investigate and planned our investigation for Monday evening, October 4th. Our host Caroline was gracious enough to let us have access to the whole castle, as there were no other guests registered for that evening. Kathy and I would be spending the night alone in a haunted castle. For most investigators, this is a dream come true. What is the ghostly legend surrounding Castle Stuart?

Reports of the castle being haunted have circulated since the 18th century, with reports of screams, voices, footsteps, moving objects and apparitions. The most haunted room in the castle is the room at the top of the east tower, currently called the Honeymoon Suite, or "Murray" room. Legend has it that a bloody apparition is sometimes seen in this room.

One of the most popular ghost stories about the castle, and this room in particular, is that of Robert Angus[65]. The Earl of Moray wanted to prove that the castle was not haunted, so he offered a reward to anyone who would spend the night in the room at the top of the east tower. Robert Angus, who people say wasn't afraid of anything, took up his offer and agreed to spend the night locked inside the castle. So, Angus was locked inside the castle by the Earl who would return the next morning to let him out. The next morning the castle was unlocked, but there was no sign of Angus anywhere. Upon entering the east tower room, the Earl and others were shocked at what was before them. The room was in complete disarray with broken glass and windows and furniture overturned and damaged as if there was some great struggle that occurred, but Angus was nowhere to be found. The "rescuers" looked out of the broken window and, to their shock, saw the lifeless body of Angus on the ground below, his face contorted in a look of horror. No one knows for sure if poor Angus was pushed out of the window or if he jumped trying to escape the horror that was inside the room. Either way it is a great story.

We began our investigation around 10:30 PM in the great hall with its polished floors of Douglas fir and walls decorated with some of the banners of clans that fought at the Battle of Culloden. What was unusual for the castle great hall was the ping pong table at the southwest end, as ping pong, or table tennis, wasn't invented until 1880. We placed a stationary video camera on the ping pong table and walked around taking photographs, EMF readings and EVP recordings. The only thing unusual that was captured in the hall was a strange "orb" that appeared in a photograph on the ping pong table. I am not a believer in orbs as the vast majority of them can be explained by dust, bugs, moisture, rain, etc., but this one was a little unusual. It almost appeared to be a ping pong ball bouncing on the ping pong table. More than likely, it is not paranormal, but it is an unusual orb. Next, we entered the billiard room, passing the billiard table to a secret doorway into the drawing room which was paneled in oak, with a grand piano, harp and large fireplace. After the drawing room, we started to investigate all of the guest bedrooms, finishing with the Honeymoon Suite, the most haunted room in the castle. There was a beautiful four-poster bed, along with a fireplace and sitting area, plus three small, round turret rooms at three corners of the bedroom. Unfortunately, we did not have any paranormal experiences during our investigation, nor did we capture anything in photographs, on audio or video that we would consider paranormal. Such is the life of a paranormal investigator. You spend hours in a location trying to capture something paranormal, only to come up empty, but I'm okay with that, especially with this investigation. At least I didn't have to jump out of a window!

Castle Stuart

At the time of this publication Castle Stuart is under new ownership and is closed due to extensive refurbishment that may take years.

Loch Ness

The next day was the day I had been waiting for all my life. I was finally going to cruise the dark waters of Loch Ness! Loch Ness[66] is the second largest lake in Scotland, almost 23 miles long, with a maximum width of almost 2 miles. It is also one of the deepest, with an average depth of 433 feet, with its deepest point 755 feet below the surface. It is also home to one of the most famous cryptids of all time, the Loch Ness Monster[67], affectionately known worldwide as "Nessie." Even though a part of me wants to believe that there is an extinct layover from the early Jurassic period some 200 million years ago swimming along the loch, another part of me doubts it. Ghosts and hauntings are easier for me to believe in, but how can we account for thousands of eyewitnesses over the years? The earliest report of the monster was written in the "Life of Columba" by Adomnán in 565 AD, which tells the story of St. Columba's encounter with the creature some 100 years earlier. No matter what I thought about the existence of Nessie, I would finally be able to see this wonderful body of water that I have read so much about. We boarded our tour boat, at the Tomnahurich Bridge in Inverness for our 5 ½ mile cruise down the Caledonian Canal into Loch Ness. Once on Loch Ness, we cruised another 7 miles to the dock at Urquhart Castle, a castle ruin dating from the 13th century, where the majority of Nessie sightings occur. I didn't see Nessie (didn't think I would) even though I kept my eyes open and my hopes up. The tour boat even had sonar on board our vessel where you could watch any "hits" in the depths on a television screen. I didn't see any "hits", but I finally accomplished a childhood dream of mine.

Photo 40 - Cruising on Loch Ness

Loch Ness
Drumnadrochit,
Loch Ness
Inverness-shire
IV63 6TU
Phone: +44 (0) 1456 450573
Website: www.lochness.com

Inverness
Visit Scotland
36 High St.0
Inverness, IV1 1JQ
Phone: 01463 252401
Website: www.visitinvernesslochness.com

Other haunted locations we visited while in Scotland included Urquhart Castle, Glencoe Valley, Culloden Battlefield, Stirling Castle and Brodie Castle. This is just a small sampling of haunted locations throughout Great Britain. We spent two splendid weeks in London and Scotland, but now it was time to come home. I had a hard time leaving as both locations were wonderful with a rich history and beauty, with some of the nicest people I have ever met.

Goodbye, Great Britain...thank you for a trip I will never forget...until next time.

Chapter Eight

THE MYRTLES PLANTATION

ONE OF AMERICA'S MOST HAUNTED HOUSES

Out of all the places I wanted to investigate, the Myrtles Plantation (photo 41) in St. Francisville, Louisiana, was number one on my list. Maybe it was because of an episode on "Unsolved Mysteries"[68] about the Myrtles in 2001 or it could have been because of the movie, "*The St. Francisville Experiment,*"[69] released in 2000, about four young people who spend the night in a haunted mansion in St. Francisville. It could have been because of a book I read in 2005 titled, "*The Myrtles Plantation: The True Story of America's Most*

Photo 41 - Myrtles Plantation

113

Haunted House," by Frances Kermeen[70], a previous owner of the Myrtles. Or better yet, maybe it was because some paranormal enthusiasts, as well as the media, have named this location as one of the most haunted houses in America. It was probably a little bit of each, but either way, this is one place I definitely wanted to check out. What makes the Myrtles Plantation one of the most haunted houses in America? Let's take a look at its history and maybe you'll understand why this beautiful and mysterious plantation home is so haunted.

The Myrtles Plantation[71], as it is known today, was built in 1796 by General David Bradford and was originally known as "Laurel Grove." General Bradford was a lawyer and prominent figure in the famous Whiskey Rebellion[72]. In 1794, he fled Washington to "Spanish West Florida" (present day Louisiana) to avoid arrest for his involvement in the rebellion. The Whiskey Rebellion was a tax protest that began in 1791 to protest a tax imposed on distilled spirits by the newly formed federal government. Since whiskey was the most popular distilled beverage in the new United States at the time, the uprising became known as the Whiskey Rebellion. The Whiskey Tax was the first tax imposed on a domestic product by the newly formed government and was the brainchild of U.S. Treasury Secretary Alexander Hamilton. The new tax was used to raise money to pay for debts incurred during the American Revolutionary War, and was eventually repealed after the Republican Party came to power in 1801. After General Bradford was pardoned in 1799 by President John Adams, he sent for his family living in Pennsylvania to join him in their new home in Louisiana.

The house was designed in the Creole-cottage style that was popular among the many plantation homes in 19th-century Louisiana. One notable feature on the outside of the home is the 125-foot-long veranda that extends along the front and southern side of the home. Today the Myrtles is a bed and breakfast with 22 rooms on two floors in the main house, with six of those rooms used as guest rooms. There are also other guest rooms around the grounds, including the Caretaker's Cottage, Coco House, garden rooms and cottages[73].

The Myrtles has had a tragic and sad history in its over 200 years of existence. In 1808, General Bradford died and the operation of the plantation was left to his widow, Elizabeth. In 1817, she turned the management of the plantation over to Judge Clarke Woodruff, who was married to her daughter Sarah Mathilda. Clarke and Sarah had three children, but tragically in 1823 and 1824, Sarah and two of their children died of yellow fever. Following Elizabeth Bradford's death in 1831, Clarke Woodruff and his one surviving daughter entrusted the management of the plantation to one of the caretakers. In 1834, the property and all of the slaves were sold to Ruffin Gray Stirling. Stirling extensively remodeled the home, doubling its size, and changed the name of the property to the Myrtles due to the many flowering crepe myrtles that grew in the vicinity.

Stirling passed away in 1854 with the property again being left to a widow. The plantation changed hands several more times in the upcoming years with more deaths occurring in and around the plantation.

Remember, this was a southern plantation in the 1800s during the time of slavery and all the pain and suffering the slaves experienced in their daily lives.

No wonder the Myrtles is as haunted as it is with all the deaths that occurred in and around the property and the suffering the slaves endured. It also doesn't help or maybe it does, depending on how you look at it, that the plantation is rumored to be built on an ancient Tunica Indian burial ground[74]. As explored in the chapter on the Signal Tree, Native American land can be extremely sacred and if Myrtles is built over a burial ground, that is all the more reason for the property to be haunted.

Besides all of the natural deaths at the plantation, there are claims that 10 murders have occurred on the property and inside the home. However, there are some experts on the history of the Myrtles who disagree on this number and believe there has been only one confirmed murder. Could there have been other murders besides the one confirmed in the Myrtles' long history? Sure, why not? For whatever reason, they may not have been documented, just passed down orally from generation to generation or maybe some were never reported at all, but just swept under the rug or made to look like an accident. It seems to me it would be very easy to get away with murder during America's infancy. In today's age, some people seem to still get away with murder, even with all of our forensics and technology, so why not back then?

In 1865, Mary Cobb, the widow of Ruffin Stirling, hired attorney William Drew Winter to help her manage her properties, which included the Myrtles. William Winter was married to Sarah Mulford, Mary Cobb's daughter, and as a show of appreciation for all of his help, Mary gave the Myrtles to William and Sarah.

One day in January 1871, William was inside the main house when he heard a rider on horseback approach the home. The unknown rider called out to William, stating he had some business with him. William went out on the side porch to speak with the man, where he was gunned down. The assailant then fled the scene on horseback and was never identified. Legend has it that William staggered back into the home, blood flowing from his wound, and slowly made his way to the staircase leading to the second floor where he died on the 17th step in the arms of his beloved wife Sarah. This makes for a great and tragic love story, especially for a beautiful location like the Myrtles, however, it is not entirely true. It has been confirmed that William Winter was shot and killed by an unknown assailant, but documentation from that time period reports William Winter died on the side porch where he succumbed to his fatal wound[75]. Who makes up these legends? Obviously, it is a much more romanticized story when someone dies in the arms of their beloved instead of dying on a porch alone.

Another story involving murder, but layered in legend, is the tale of "Chloe."[76] Legend has it that Clarke Woodruff had sexual affairs with his female slaves, including a household slave named Chloe who has also been known as Cleo. Chloe hated being the object of Woodruff's advances, but she didn't want to return to work in the fields, so she learned to live with them.

After time, Woodruff grew tired of Chloe and found another slave to satisfy his desires. Chloe became concerned that her fears of returning to the fields would soon come true, so she started eavesdropping on Woodruff's conversations to see what he had in store for her. One day in 1817, Woodruff caught her listening at the door and, to teach her a lesson, ordered to have one of her ears cut off. From that day forward, Chloe always wore a green turban to cover her disfigurement. What happened next is unclear, but it is said that Chloe poisoned Woodruff's wife Sarah and two of his three children. It was the oldest daughter's birthday so Chloe decided to bake a birthday cake for her, but it was no ordinary birthday cake -- Chloe added crushed oleander flowers to the recipe. Some speculate that Chloe killed them for revenge; others think she just wanted to make them sick so she could nurse them back to health to earn the judge's good graces. Whatever the reason, three members of Woodruff's family were now dead.

Once the other slaves heard what happened, they took matters into their own hands. Fearful that Woodruff would punish all of them for his loved ones' deaths, they dragged Chloe screaming from her bed and hanged her from a nearby tree. After she was dead, they took her body to the Mississippi River less than three miles away where they tied rocks to her body and threw it into the river. Ever since, the ghost of Chloe has been seen roaming the plantation grounds.

This is another great story, but is it based on fact or fiction? There are many people who believe the story and believe in the ghost of Chloe, but just like other legends, this story is not based in fact and again there is no written record that these tragic events actually happened. As stated earlier in this chapter, Sarah Woodruff and two of their children died of yellow fever in 1823 and 1824, which is based on fact and *has* been documented. So, based on these documents, they could not have died by poisoning six years earlier in 1817. Does it really matter if they were murdered or not? Regardless, they all died tragically. Besides all the deaths that have occurred on the property, there is also a long history of sadness, pain and despair. You don't need much more than that for a location to be haunted. But what of Chloe? Did she really exist? Let's just say there has been no documented records of Clarke Woodruff ever owning a slave girl named Chloe or Cleo.

I first visited and investigated the Myrtles in June 2011. My wife Kathy had business in New Orleans and I usually accompanied her on her business trips. Since we were going to an entertaining and historical city like New Orleans, we invited my sister Shelley and her husband Jim to join us. Shelley loves delving into the paranormal and going on investigations so she jumped at the chance.

Jim, on the other hand, does not and thinks it is all a bunch of nonsense even though he still goes along for the ride. I was praying he would have a frightening experience at the Myrtles just to shut him up. If you know Jim, you know what I'm talking about.

We flew into New Orleans from St. Louis, Missouri, where we were visiting Shelley and Jim prior to this trip. We stayed at the Hilton New Orleans Riverside, situated right alongside the Mississippi River in the heart of New Orleans. We only stayed in New Orleans for a couple days while Kathy took care of business. After exploring Bourbon Street, the Garden District and two breathtaking and historic and haunted cemeteries, St. Louis Cemetery No. 1 and Lafayette Cemetery No. 1, we rented a car and drove two hours northwest to St. Francisville and the Myrtles Plantation.

As we started driving up the driveway, I could barely contain myself, as this is something I wanted to do for a long time. Kathy, on the other hand, didn't feel quite as enthusiastic and was very apprehensive about the whole thing, which I did not understand. She is a paranormal investigator, yet it took me some time to convince her to travel to the Myrtles and spend the night. For some reason, there was something about this place that made her uneasy. Prior to this trip, she had spent nights investigating places like: The Queen Mary – Long Beach, CA (May 2005); The Watseka Wonder House – Watseka, IL (December 2005); The Lemp Mansion – St. Louis, MO (August 2007); 800-year-old haunted castles – Scotland (September and October 2010) and the Jerome Grand Hotel – Jerome, AZ (March 2011). So, what was it about the Myrtles that made her so nervous? She did not have an answer.

I was in awe as we drove down the tree-lined driveway to the parking area. We parked, got out and just stood there looking at the house and grounds, which were beautiful. There was a large brick

Photo 42 - Author and Kathy at the Myrtles Plantation

patio situated in front of us and directly behind the main house. Across the patio was the general store that contained a gift shop and check-in. To our left was the Carriage House Restaurant. Farther back on the property were several guest cottages.

We checked in and received our keys. Shelley and Jim were in the General David Bradford Suite located on the first floor in the main house. Their exterior door led right onto the brick patio. Kathy and I stayed in the Judge Clark Woodruff Suite on the second floor in the main house. Our room was more removed from the other rooms and when you think about it, this makes the room a little creepier.

To get to the Woodruff Suite, you had to enter a large foyer (photo 43) through a private door on the southwest side of the house and then take the stairs to the second floor, the same stairs where legend says William Winter died. The door to the Woodruff Suite is located near the top of the stairs. There are four other bedrooms in the main house, but they are located on the opposite side of the house with their own private entrance. We were the only guests who had keys to this side of the house. If we needed to run out of the house, for whatever reason, no other guests would hear or see us. That could be a bad thing or a good thing!

We spent the rest of the day exploring and getting to know the grounds. If the story of Chloe was true, we wondered which tree she was hanged from. We thought of what life must have been like back then, which was easy to do because the area lacked the modern sounds

Photo 43 - Myrtles main house foyer

of automobile traffic. The only sounds were the wind blowing in the trees and the birds and insects singing and chirping the day away. The only modern reminder of the 21st century was the cars parked in the parking lot. Whenever we went someplace I always tried to imagine what the property and/or buildings looked like 100, 500, 1,000 years ago and even longer.

Since this was our first time here, we signed up for a tour of the house that would be held that evening. We had some time to spare prior to the tour so we went out to grab a bite to eat and returned just in time. Other guests of the Myrtles who would be on the tour that evening included a family of four and three women who were staying in the Caretaker's Cottage. Our guide gave us a history and ghost tour of the outside and inside of the property. One of the things the tour guide showed and talked about was the "haunted" mirror (photo 44) that hung in the main foyer of the main house -- the same mirror we had to pass to go to our room. This large mirror is said to contain the spirits of Sarah Woodruff and her two children. Some religions believe when someone dies all of the mirrors in the house

Photo 44 - The "haunted" mirror

where they passed need to be covered to prevent the deceased person's soul from becoming trapped inside the glass. It is also a belief that after death, evil spirits and demons can use uncovered mirrors as a portal to enter the house of the living to fill the void left by the deceased individual's soul. There are several other reasons why mirrors are covered, but in the case of the mirror at the Myrtles, these seem to be the accepted reasons.

Legend has it that when Sarah and her children died, all of the mirrors in the house were covered except this one. Why, no one knows for sure, but many visitors and employees claim to see handprints in the mirror that are attributed to Sarah and her children, as well as others who have died at the plantation. The mirrors have been cleaned repeatedly and even the glass in this mirror has been replaced, but the handprints still reappear. Some skeptics believe the handprints are actually in the wood behind the mirror and not in the glass itself. Whatever the reason, we did observe something that appeared to be a handprint in the glass.

During the rest of the tour, we were fascinated with other facts and legends about the Myrtles, including William Winter's murder.

After the tour, we decided it was time to conduct our own paranormal investigation. Kathy, Shelley and I gathered our gear, which included a video camera, digital camera, EMF detectors and a digital voice audio recorder. Jim, being a non-believer, sat this investigation out, opting to sit on the patio chatting with the other guests, some whom were now a little bit apprehensive about sleeping at the Myrtles, especially after hearing all of the paranormal stories during the tour.

We started our investigation in Shelley's bedroom, the General David Bradford Suite. We stayed in that room for a while, but since there didn't seem to be any activity going on, we moved into the main foyer where the haunted mirror was located. We investigated the first and second floors along with the staircase, and placed equipment all over, including a video camera focused on the stairs with an EMF detector situated on the 17th step (photo 45) in an attempt to capture any type of paranormal activity. I wandered around the first and

Photo 45 - The 17th step

second floors, taking a lot of photographs, including photos of the mirror that still showed the handprints. Kathy was using her audio recorder for an EVP session on the first floor sitting on the stairs near a baby grand piano (photo 46). During the session, she asked the questions, "Do you know whose piano this is?" and "Who used to play it?" After the second question, a possible EVP was captured in which a male's voice said, "I did."

Photo 46 - Kathy doing an EVP session

After investigating the two floors of the main house, we decided to head outside toward the area of the Caretaker's Cottage. Once we went outside, the three female guests who were staying in the cottage decided they were now brave enough to join us, which left Jim all by himself. Since Jim had no one to talk with anymore, he decided to head back to his room and go to bed. All of us, including the three women, hoped he would get the crap scared out of him!

We wandered the grounds attempting to capture audio, video or photographic evidence, but the sounds of the chirping and singing insects drowned out all possible EVPs. Something did happen while we were outside that scared the living daylights out of us, something we could find no logical explanation.

The Caretaker's Cottage (photo 47) is located about 40 yards north of the main house and is surrounded by a wooden fence and gate. All of us had just finished investigating inside the cottage and were standing outside the fence and gate with the gate standing open. The gate was hard to open and close because the bottom of the gate dragged on the brick and stone walkway that was imbedded in the ground. We placed our video camera, which was on a tripod, on the ground just outside of the fence, facing the main house. The six of us were standing around chatting when all of a sudden, "BAM," the gate slammed shut with such force that we all did a hop, skip and a jump! It scared the living

Photo 47 - The Caretaker's Cottage and gate

daylights out of us! We all turned around and observed the gate now closed! The gate was definitely open when we went through and it was definitely stuck on the ground -- of we were 100% sure. Whatever closed the gate used a tremendous amount of force and energy to slam it as hard as it did. I tried to recreate the slamming of the gate, but with the gate stuck on the ground, it took a little effort on my part to close it. If only I had the video camera directed at the gate instead of the house. I spent the rest of the night trying to debunk and recreate it, wondering what the hell caused the gate to slam shut, but could come up with no logical explanation. It was now around 3:00 AM, so we all decided to end the investigation and go to bed, except for our three female guests. They were now terrified and decided they would not be able to go to sleep, so they decided they were going to stay up for the rest of the night and get an early start in the morning to head back home. I have to admit, I was also a little nervous about sleeping in our room. There was something about this place that put fear in me, but I could not put my finger on why, because I have slept in some really haunted places before and never had a problem. I imagined myself sleeping and being woken by some strange noise from a far-off corner of the room. I would then slowly and reluctantly open my eyes, only to discover an unearthly presence standing right next to my bed, staring into my soul. Imagine lying in bed and opening your eyes to see a face staring back at you or being in bed and having the covers ripped off you! How about hanging your foot or hand over the side of the bed and some cold, boney hand grabbing it. Those are some scenarios I have always feared as a child and now those thoughts were racing through my mind.

Kathy and I returned to our bedroom and Shelley returned to hers where Jim was soundly asleep. We prepared for bed, placing a video camera in a corner of the room to capture anything unusual during the night. I checked under the bed, but there was nothing there, and turned on my sound machine extra loud. I like the sound of crickets to help me sleep. As usual, Kathy was asleep in a matter of minutes, but not me. Sometimes I would lie in bed a good while with thoughts, ideas and worries of the day and upcoming days. This night, I laid in bed, glancing around the room every so often, and eventually fell asleep. The next morning, I woke up and discovered I made it through the night. No faces or apparitions messed with me last night. Both my wife and I survived the night at the Myrtles Plantation.

We packed up and made our way back to New Orleans where we caught our flight home.

Once home I reviewed the video camera we had set up in our room. Nothing.

Besides the gate slamming, we really did not have any other personal experiences, but all in all, we had a fantastic and frightful time at the Myrtles.

The Myrtles Plantation has been featured on *Unsolved Mysteries*, *Ghost Hunters*, *Ghost Adventures* and *Most Terrifying Places in America* and is listed on the National Register of Historic Places.

If you are looking for that place with a spooky ambiance and a sad and tragic past, I would highly recommend the Myrtles Plantation in St. Francisville, Louisiana. I just hope you have a good night's sleep!

Myrtles Plantation
7747 U.S. Highway 61
P.O. Box 1100
St. Francisville, Louisiana 70775
Phone: 225-635-6277 and 800-809-0565
Website: www.myrtlesplantation.com.

Chapter Nine

<u>THE ROADS HOTEL</u>

ROARING 20s COME BACK TO LIFE

Imagine if you could travel back in time to the 1920s and 1930s during the Prohibition era when it was illegal to produce, import, transport, sell or consume alcohol. If you could, you would be living in the world of bootlegging, gangsters, brothels and speakeasies. There is a place in Atlanta, Indiana, where the hands of time take you back to that troublesome and violent era in American history. That place is the historic and haunted Roads Hotel (photo 48).

Photo 48 - The Roads Hotel

Atlanta, Indiana, is located approximately 35 miles north of Indianapolis and was originally known as Sheilville, after Ireland-born General Michael Sheil who settled in the area in 1834[77].

There were very few settlers in the area in 1834, so in 1836, Sheil constructed a trading post to conduct transactions with the local Native American tribe, the Miami.

In 1846, a small town sprang up next to Sheilville called Buena Vista. Also, in 1846, the Peru & Indianapolis Railroad selected Buena Vista to lay their tracks connecting Indianapolis with the Wabash and Erie Canal. Thus, began the decline of Sheilville in 1854 when the tracks were finally laid. In 1885, Buena Vista was renamed Atlanta since a larger community in Indiana called Buena Vista had already been established. Some say the name Atlanta was chosen after the city of the same name in Georgia, whose beauty was described by soldiers returning from the Civil War.

Atlanta, Indiana, was a boom town in the late 1800s and early 1900s due to the discovery of gas wells in the vicinity. Because of these wells, numerous businesses sprang up, employing some 2,000 employees by the turn of the century. Things were looking good for the small town, but in the 1930s, the wells went dry and the once bustling town was no more. As of the 2010 census, the population of Atlanta, Indiana, was 725[78].

The Roads Hotel was built in 1893 during those prosperous years at the end of the 19th century and is currently listed on the National Register of Historic Places. For most of its existence, except for a short time when it was turned into apartments in the 1970s, it has been used as a hotel.

The two-story hotel is designed in the Queen Anne style, with an ornate two-story front porch. There is also an attic with a widow's walk on the roof.

After the hotel was built, Newton Roads, the hotel's namesake, purchased the building for his wife Clara Roads. Newton and Clara had two children, a son Everett, 3, and a daughter Hazel, 7, when they moved into the hotel.

A year after moving into the hotel, Everett was diagnosed with whooping cough, leaving the boy with asthma. When Everett was 18 years old, he contracted tuberculosis. The family did what they could and what they thought was right in treating Everett's disease, but back then, treatment for tuberculosis was plenty of rest, a proper diet and isolation. Everett was confined to an area of the hotel away from others in the hope he would recover. No matter what Newton and Clara did, they could not save their son. Everett died six months following his diagnosis on April 15, 1909, at the young age of 19. As was customary in those days, Everett was laid out in the parlor of the hotel for family and friends to pay their last respects.

When Hazel was old enough, she helped her mother operate the hotel. On August 25, 1913, Hazel married Harry Meehan in the hotel and later had a son named William.

There were a few other deaths in the Roads family in addition to Everett's untimely passing in the hotel. On January 22, 1926, Newton Roads passed away at the age of 65. He too was laid out in the hotel so family and friends could pay their last respects. Clara Roads passed away in the hotel at the age of 79 on February 5, 1941. She had been sick for quite a while when she fell and broke her hip, which eventually led to her passing. Hazel lived with her mother, taking care of her until her death. Hazel passed away after a short illness on January 28, 1968, at the age of 81 in a nursing home in Elwood, Indiana. Her body was laid out at the Atlanta Methodist Church, across the street from the hotel, where family and friends paid their last respects[79].

During the Prohibition era between 1920 and 1933, the hotel was used as a speakeasy and brothel. It is told that several murders, assaults and abortions took place inside the hotel, but these stories have not been confirmed. It is also rumored that the aborted fetuses were buried in the basement, which has since been filled in. Legend has it that Al Capone and John Dillinger patronized the hotel during their gangster and bank robbing days[80], which doesn't seem out of the question considering they terrorized the Midwest. In fact, John Dillinger robbed seven banks in Indiana, including the Commercial Bank in Daleville, Indiana, only about 25 miles east of the Roads Hotel, on July 17, 1933[81].

I have visited and investigated the Roads Hotel twice, once in May 2016 and again in September of that same year.

The first time I visited the hotel was with several members of Tri-C Ghost Hunters, a paranormal team from Ohio, of which I am a co-founder. We attended a small event that was held there with other friends and investigators.

We drove through the town and I would have to say it was one of the smallest towns I have ever visited. I believe there was one restaurant called The Pub and a Dollar General on the main route just outside of town. Other than that, there was not much else. During the day, it is a quiet little town, but at night, it seemed to take on an eerie stillness. I remember standing outside the hotel at night getting fresh air, but there was not even a breeze. There seemed to be no sounds at all, not even the sounds of crickets or other creatures of the night.

That first time, we stayed two nights and had the opportunity to investigate both nights. At the time, you could rent out the entire hotel for the weekend. There were eight bedrooms and two bathrooms on the second floor. On the first floor, there was another bedroom and a full bathroom, as well as a full kitchen.

Photo 49 - Second floor hallway

During our stay, just about everyone staying at the hotel had some sort of paranormal encounter. Shadows were seen in the second-floor hallway (photo 49). Several guests were touched or had their hair pulled. Others smelled strange odors, heard odd noises or had a feeling of apprehension while inside the hotel. There were two harrowing encounters that stood out from the rest during that first night's investigation. The first encounter occurred while my wife Kathy and I were investigating the second floor. We were investigating one of the eight bedrooms located on that floor when we heard a strange noise coming from one of the bedrooms toward the front of the hotel. We were the only ones on the second floor at the time. The noise sounded like a loud thump, as if something had fallen. I told Kathy I would go check it out and walked down the hallway to the front of the hotel while she stayed in one of the rooms conducting an EVP session (photo 50). Once I arrived at the end of the hall, I stood still and listened. It was eerily quiet. I walked into the bedroom on the right, listening for anything paranormal or natural. Again, it was quiet. I walked back across the short hall into the other bedroom, which was known as the Madam's bedroom. I again stood and

listened intently for a few moments and, like the previous room, it was quiet and still. As I walked out the bedroom (photo 51), I felt an intense burning sensation across my throat, I screamed in pain and immediately grabbed for my throat. It felt as

Photo 50 - Kathy investigating one of the bedrooms

if my throat had been cut with a knife! I have never had my throat cut, but if I did, I imagine it would feel like this! My wife came running and found me grabbing my throat. "What's wrong?" she kept asking. All I could do was look at her with a shocked look in my eyes, helplessly gasping, while still holding my throat. Eventually the pain subsided and I was able to explain to her what happened. Was this something residual I was feeling? Was someone attacked with a knife and possibly murdered in the past in the exact same spot or was I physically attacked by some vengeful and angry ghost, something that

Photo 51 - Doorway to Madam's bedroom

took offense to me being in "their" room, even the Madam herself? Whatever the reason, it scared the crap out of me and I still had to sleep two nights in the hotel!

The next paranormal experience took place in the attic several hours later. There is a story told of a man who committed suicide by hanging himself in the attic. According to the story, the man was a preacher who became despondent over his frequent visits to the brothel and speakeasy. In his despaired state, he climbed the stairs to the widow's walk, put a noose around his neck and jumped through the opening into the attic, killing himself.

Five of us including my wife Kathy, Todd a Tri-C Ghost Hunter member, two friends, Tess and Katona, and I decided to go into the attic to investigate.

The attic was dark with some outside ambient light permeating the darkness, creating eerie shadows on the attic walls and ceiling. The unfinished attic had collected layers of dust over the years. There were a few boxes and other discarded items lying about, such as a couple of mattresses, old windows and Christmas decorations. At one end of the attic were the steps that led up to the widow's walk where the preacher had committed suicide (photo 52).

Photo 52 – Ladder leading to the widow walk

We arranged ourselves in a semi-circle in the center of the attic near the stairs leading down to the floor below, with Todd, Tess, Katona,

Kathy and myself in that order. I was sitting on a chair on Kathy's right side with a digital camera in my right hand and a KII EMF meter in my left. Everyone else was standing. I placed a digital audio recorder in the center of the attic so we could contact the preacher through an EVP session. Things started out quietly, but after a short time, we started to hear distinct footsteps walking around us in the far corners of the attic. The footsteps could be heard walking one way, turn around and then start walking the other way. It felt as if some carnivore, such as a tiger or wolf, was stalking its prey and we were the prey. We all started feeling a little nervous when all of a sudden, I felt a sharp pain in my chest. I gasped, but before I could say anything, Kathy relayed that she was experiencing a pain in her chest. Then Tess stated she was feeling the same type of pain! This was getting crazy! Three of us were having chest pains at the same time with no logical explanation. Right then, Kathy felt someone or something standing right behind her. She was frozen in fear, as she could feel heavy breathing on the back of her neck. "Who's behind me?" she asked, thinking one of us was standing behind her, but it was not any of us. I turned on my flashlight and started taking photographs behind her (photo 53), but there was nothing there that

we could see. Then without warning, Kathy let out a blood-curdling scream that made the rest of us jump out of our skins! Kathy asked me in a shaky and highly agitated voice, "Did you do that!?!?" I had no idea what

Photo 53 – Nothing behind Kathy

135

she was talking about. All she kept saying was "Did you do that!?!? Did you do that!?!?" After she calmed down, she explained that something had grabbed her right shoulder and started to squeeze down with such force that she screamed out in pain and fear. When she was finished telling us what happened, Todd, who was standing near the stairs, explained after Kathy screamed, he felt a rush of air that raced passed him down the stairs that startled him. It looks like Kathy not only scared the crap out of us with her scream, but also scared whatever or whoever grabbed her too!

One last frightening experience I had at the Roads Hotel was when we returned with other members of Tri-C Ghost Hunters a few months later in September.

As mentioned earlier, the cool thing about investigating the Roads Hotel, was groups could rent out the hotel and spend the entire weekend there, which we did again when we visited the second time.

The first time we visited the hotel, Kathy and I stayed in one of the bedrooms at the far end of the second-floor hallway. On this visit, however, my wife decided she wanted to sleep in the Madam's bedroom at the front of the hotel. Wonderful -- the same room where I had my throat slashed and that's the room she wants to spend a couple nights in?!? Did she forget what happened to me on the prior investigation? Oh well, why not, I thought, besides there is no way anything like that would happen again…wrong!

We arrived at the hotel in the early afternoon. Everyone was in a great mood, but after a while, moods started to change following a huge argument between a couple of people. This also happened the last time we were there in May when an argument broke out between several people. We have been to the Roads Hotel twice and each time, temperaments have changed. This has never happened at any other location we have investigated. It might be something to be aware of if you ever decide to visit the Roads Hotel.

After we arrived, I took our bags upstairs to the Madam's room (photo 54). I stood outside the door, somewhat apprehensive about entering. I finally got up the courage to enter and placed our bags on the bed. No physical attacks -- maybe I would be okay staying and sleeping in this bedroom. Throughout the day I would enter and exit the bedroom several times with no problems.

Photo 54 - Madam's bedroom

Around 1:30 AM, all of us had retired for the night after a full evening of investigating. I had no trouble falling asleep as I felt very comfortable in the room now. I was asleep for several hours when I was suddenly awakened by a sharp, stabbing and burning sensation on the right side of my abdomen. Not again! I clutched my side and screamed out in pain, waking Kathy. She felt helpless as there was nothing she could do to ease the pain. After a short while, the pain finally subsided, but I was now beginning to think maybe it was not residual at all. Maybe it *was* the Madam and she was not too enthusiastic about me sleeping in *her* bedroom. I had a hard time falling back to sleep for fear that I would experience the attack again My eyes grew so heavy, though, that I eventually drifted back to sleep. Thankfully, there were no other attacks during the night, but I still had to sleep in Madam's room one more night and was dreading it. If I could have, I would have slept in another room, but all of the bedrooms were occupied.

I was now fearful of the coming night and was nervous about sleeping in Madam's room again. Prior to going to bed that second night, I decided to see if I could reason with the Madam. I explained that I was not there to harm her in any way and pleaded and begged for her not to hurt me anymore. It must have worked because she left me alone. I slept soundly and comfortably the second night. Madam, I thank you!

As of this writing, the Roads Hotel is under new ownership. For information on investigating, staying and other events at the Roads Hotel, please visit their website.

The Roads Hotel
150 E. Main Street
Atlanta, Indiana 46031
Phone: 317-832-7692
Website: www.rhoadshotel.com

Chapter Ten

ST. JOSEPH HOSPITAL

STILL CARING FOR THEIR PATIENTS

St. Joseph Hospital had always been a hive of activity ever since it opened its doors over 126 years ago with doctors and nurses making their rounds, taking care of the many patients throughout the hospital. Ambulances pulling up to the emergency room doors, employees registering patients, food workers preparing the many meals that were needed, gift shop workers, office workers and janitors, plus many, many others. Family and friends visiting patients, of which some would go home and others who never would. There was laughter, joy, relief, anger and sorrow. Nowadays there is none of that at the abandoned hospital. There are no more doctors, nurses and employees rushing about doing their jobs helping others. There are no more patients lying in bed wondering if they will ever get to go home again. Injured or sick patients are no longer being rushed to the emergency room to receive life-saving treatment. All of that is gone...or is it?

St. Joseph Hospital had a humble beginning when it first opened in a house in Lorain, Ohio, in 1892[82]. Father Joseph L. Bihn, Sister Mary Ludmilla Schmidt and Sister Mary Antonia Adams decided that a hospital was needed in Lorain for children who required immediate care as the closest hospital was about 20 miles away in Cleveland. Father Bihn had a love for children, especially those in need, such as the injured, sick and orphaned. In 1867 while he was the pastor of St. Joseph Catholic Church in Tiffin, Ohio, he dreamed of establishing a home for orphans and the elderly in Tiffin. His

139

dream came true on June 4, 1869, when the first orphans and adults were admitted into what became known as The Citizens Hospital and Orphan Asylum, where orphaned children lived until 1936[83]. Today the facility still cares for older adults and is known as the St. Francis Home. If it wasn't for his devotion to children and helping others, there would be no St. Francis Home or St. Joseph Hospital.

Lorain, Ohio, originally called Black River Township, was first settled in 1807 on the shores of Lake Erie at the mouth of the Black River. Lorain County, in which the City of Lorain is located, received its name from the Province of Lorraine, France. In 1763, Lorain County was originally a portion of French Canada, hence the name New France. Lorain was incorporated as a village in 1873.

In 1890, the population of Lorain was 4,863 residents, but by 1910, the population skyrocketed to 28,883 residents[84]. That is almost a 494% increase in only 20 years! Due to this population explosion within the community, St. Joseph Hospital needed to expand as well to keep up with the ever-increasing demand for medical care as it was turning into a full-fledged hospital treating both children and adults. In 1901, an organized medical staff was added to St. Joseph Hospital and in 1903, the hospital averaged 25 patients a day. Construction of a new St. Joseph Hospital, located at the southwest corner of Broadway and W. 21st Street, was completed in 1916. The population of Lorain continued to grow due to the booming steel industry in Lorain, which included the Ford Motor Company, Lorain Assembly plant and the United States Steel mill. In 1950, the population of Lorain was 51,202, another 77% increase. Because of this growth, St. Joseph Hospital needed to expand again, this time to a more modern 100,000- square-foot facility that was completed in 1950 (photo 55). The population of Lorain reached its peak in 1970 with 78,185 residents, but has been in steady decline since the closing of the assembly plant and steel mill. The 2017 population is estimated at 63,841[85], which still makes Lorain around the 10th largest city in Ohio.

In 1993, St. Joseph Hospital merged with Lorain Community Hospital, which opened in 1964. In 1997, St. Joseph Hospital closed its doors forever after serving the community for 105 years and moved to its new location, a new modern facility at 3700 Kolbe Road, Lorain, where it is now known as Mercy Regional Medical Center.

Photo 55 - St. Joseph Hospital, Lorain, Ohio

Tragedy struck the City of Lorain on Saturday evening June 28, 1924, when a massive tornado hit the city without warning. It was a day just like any other warm summer day in Lorain with people going about their daily lives, but then day turned into night and carefreeness turned to horror a little after 5:00 PM as a huge tornado, estimated to be an F-4, walloped into the heart of the city, packing 207 to 260 MPH winds. Over 35 blocks, including about 500 homes and many businesses, were destroyed, all from a storm lasting roughly 20 minutes. Some 1,000 additional homes and businesses suffered varying degrees of structural damage. Over 200 people were injured, many of them critically, but the biggest loss was the 72 people who perished in the storm, with the majority of them dying in the tornado's path along Broadway, Lorain's main business district. This was the deadliest and most destructive tornado to ever strike the state of Ohio[86].

There were not enough medical professionals in Lorain at the time, so countless doctors and hundreds of nurses rushed in from Cleveland and the surrounding areas to help with the hundreds of injured. Many of the injured and dying were taken to St. Joseph Hospital, the only hospital in Lorain at the time.

Several of the businesses along Broadway are alleged to be haunted. One of those is the Lorain Palace Theater, which was constructed in 1928 to replace the State Theater that was destroyed during the tornado. Fifteen people were killed inside the State Theater, along with numerous injured. In fact, my team, Tri-C Ghost Hunters, has investigated several businesses along Broadway, including the Lorain Palace Theater.

I first heard about St. Joseph Hospital and it possibly being haunted in October 2015, the same month that the original 1916 portion of the hospital, called Building D, was being torn down. Apparently, the old hospital became unsafe with rotting floors and unstable walls. The main part of the hospital, which was still standing, was vacant with only the Veterans' Administration using a portion of the hospital on the first floor. In recent years, portions of the hospital had been used for county offices and a local college used some of the rooms for its nursing classes, but the majority of the hospital had not been used since it closed in 1997. Former employees would say the hospital was haunted even when it was still in operation. The hospital had never been investigated before and I knew someone who could get us in.

It seems almost every hospital, open or closed, has a few ghost stories that are passed around by former employees who talk of phantom nurses, doctors and patients, and St. Joseph Hospital was no exception. Throughout St. Joseph's history, nuns, some of whom had nursing degrees, could be seen walking the floors offering comfort and spiritual healing to the many patients. In the early days of the hospital, the nuns wore habits and hats called a cornette, which was white with large prominent "wings" or "horns." In later years, the nuns started dressing more casually, making it more difficult to distinguish the nuns from the nurses.

One of the stories from St. Joseph is about the ghost a nun who had been observed by past patients and employees walking the halls and tending to patients' needs. Many patients who were scared and alone would see a young nun dressed in a full habit sitting on the edge of the hospital bed, giving them comfort and hope. One particular story about the nun comes from one night in the early 1990s. A former nurse was making her rounds, checking on patients before the end of her shift. She went into one patient's room and asked if he required anything before she left. He responded, "No, the sister has been with me for the last hour." The nurse was confused as this patient had no visitors during her shift, especially a nun, which she would have remembered. She told the patient, "I have been here all day and you have had no visitor, sir." The patient was very adamant that he had a visitor and was looking forward to seeing her again. Becoming perplexed, the nurse started asking other coworkers about this strange occurrence. To her surprise, the mysterious nun had been observed on other occasions by patients who were all alone and had no one to visit or comfort them. The spectral nun had been seen by too many patients for it to be a coincidence or a dream. The hospital is closed and all of the patient rooms are now empty, but the nun is still there making her rounds to comfort unseen patients.

Another tale is of a new unit secretary starting her first day on the job who was very nervous with her new responsibilities, but she was very happy with her newly acquired position. Her new position required her to sit at a desk at the nurses' station on a patient wing of the hospital. From her desk, she had a clear view down the hall to the patient rooms. Every so often, she would look up from her desk to see nurses going in and out of patient rooms. One time when she looked up, something caught her attention that seemed strange and out of place. Down the hall, she observed a young nurse with her blond hair neatly pinned to her white nurses' cap dressed in a white, neatly pressed nurses' uniform that extended below her knees. Her uniform didn't match the other nurses, but seemed from an earlier time period. When their eyes locked, the young nurse warmly waved and then slowly disappeared, like she was never there!

There have been other stories passed on about this young nurse, with many employees and patients seeing her on several floors of the hospital. One story told is about a patient who pushed the nurse call button for assistance. When the nurse was finally able to answer the call, the now-frightened patient told her there was another nurse in the room just before her, however, she had no visible legs from the knees down.

While interviewing former nurses who used to work at the hospital, I was told in 1981 a young nurse by the name of Linda was killed in a traffic accident while on her way to work. Linda never really had a family of her own and working at the hospital was her life. Coworkers and patients had essentially become her family. Was Linda still making her rounds after her life was tragically cut short? It sure seems like it to me.

Other tragic and sad deaths have occurred inside the hospital besides the death of the young nurse and the countless others who have died in the hospital. There is the untimely passing of one of the hospital's doctors in the early 1990s. Nurses had spent some time trying to contact the doctor through the telephone and his pager, to no avail. Finally, one of the nurses was sent to look for him and discovered him dead of natural causes on the second floor near what is now the old labor and delivery area.

Sometime in the 1980s, a man committed suicide by jumping from the top level of the parking garage, landing on the roof of the first floor. Numerous patients and employees witnessed this horrific spectacle.

I was also told by several former nurses about the patient in the burn ward who was burned over 75% of his body from a farming accident. He passed away in room 541. Out of all the patients they cared for over the years, this one left a sad impression on them that they will never forget.

After the hospital closed in 1997, security guards and maintenance workers who still worked inside the old building relayed their encounters with the paranormal and ghosts of the hospital. One security guard said he and a partner were walking through the old psychiatric ward on the third floor when they discovered a male intruder. They yelled at him and gave chase as he took off running down the hallway. The unknown man came upon some double-doors with glass windows, but instead of opening the doors, the man went right through them as if they were not there (photo 56). Upon this change of events, the security guards decided they had enough and turned around and ran the other way. Looking behind them as they ran, they saw the man grinning at them through the glass windows!

Photo 56 - Double doors in psychiatric ward

Since security guards were often in the building alone, they saw and heard a lot of things they could not explain. One security guard, while making her rounds on the patient floors, closed all of the curtains that were still hanging in each room. When she returned to make another round, all the curtains were open again.

One of the more unusual occurrences happened in the original 1916 building, Building D. The local police department received a desperate emergency call from a pregnant woman stranded in one of the elevators. The police department contacted the hospital security guard on duty and advised her of the situation. The guard proceeded to check all the elevators, but could find no one stranded. All the elevators were functioning normally, even though police dispatch was still on the phone with the woman who was growing increasingly frantic. The security guard could actually hear the woman pleading for help through the dispatcher's phone. The most bizarre thing about this incident was Building D had already been closed for several years and no one should have been inside the building.

I first met Bill in early October 2015. Bill has worked at St. Joseph Hospital since 1996 and is the maintenance supervisor in charge of the daily upkeep of the building. Bill was the person who could allow us inside the hospital to investigate. The first time I met Bill, he was decent enough to give me a tour of the hospital, which looked to be in pretty good shape for a building that has been closed since 1997. It had everything you think of when you think of hospitals -- four patient floors, which included throughout its history orthopedics, labor and delivery, pediatrics, hospice, psychiatric ward, drug outpatient rehab center, plastic surgery, burn unit, geriatrics, maternity and oncology. There was a chapel, cafeteria, kitchen, gift shop, surgical, recovery room, ICU/CCU, a morgue and ER, plus many support offices. In addition to the main building, there was a VA Center and medical center that were still being used. There was also a basement and large auditorium where lectures were given. This place was huge and it was very easy to get lost in its maze of hallways, stairs and rooms. Bill relayed several strange things he has experienced while working inside the hospital with doors slamming being the most common. Even though there were a couple other maintenance guys working at the hospital, most of the time Bill would be in the massive, empty building alone. He would be walking down one of the quiet patient floors checking on things when doors would start slamming behind him. Of course, it startled him, as it would startle me, but he always figured there must be someone else on the floor messing with him and nothing paranormal in nature. He would turn around and search the entire floor, but could never find anyone. This happened to him more than a few times over the years and always on the second and third patient floors.

Harold, another employee who has worked in preventive maintenance for St. Joseph Hospital since about 2008, has also had

147

several paranormal experiences within the hospital walls. Harold stated one day he and a security guard were sitting in the maintenance office chatting. The office consisted of a main room with several small adjoining offices, some with windows into the main office. There was only one door into the main office from the hallway. Harold was sitting in a chair just under one of the windows and near the only entrance. While the two were chatting, something started banging on the window directly behind Harold. Both of them flew out of their chairs, shouting a few choice words. They searched the office for the funny prankster, but they found no one else inside the office with them, at least no living person.

Some of the areas Harold does not like inside the hospital are the ER and a wing of the fourth floor. In fact, former nurses who worked at the hospital told me that more deaths occurred on the fourth floor, formerly the geriatric floor, than any other place in the hospital.

The area that Harold hated the most was the basement. Witnesses have reported seeing shadowy figures and the apparition of an elderly gentleman wearing a Cleveland Indians baseball jacket down in the basement. Harold relayed one time he was in the basement doing routine maintenance when he heard his name called out three times, "Harold...Harold...Harold." He assumed it was the security guard looking for him, but when he responded, he was greeted with silence. Again, he responded, still no answer. He then radioed the security guard to see if he was in the basement looking for him. The guard radioed back that he was not in the basement and was in another part of the hospital. That was enough to freak Harold out and he quickly left the basement. Other suspicious activity from the basement included loud banging noises as if someone was using a hammer to strike a pipe and the sighting of a ghostly, transparent figure working on a heating tank in the boiler room.

The strangest and most chilling paranormal incident involved two workers who were near the emergency room. Harold relayed the story of outside workers hired to replace drywall and repair an electrical box in a maintenance closet in the old radiology room adjacent to the ER. The two workers were inside the closet working on the panel when they heard giggling coming from the radiology room. They turned around, looked out into the room and saw two young boys standing there laughing at them. Since the hospital had been closed for some time and there were hazards inside the building, the workers yelled at the boys, asking what they were doing inside the building. The boys said nothing, but continued laughing as they turned and ran out of the room. The two workers gave chase, following the boys down a short hallway and through the old emergency room where the boys darted into another room. The workers were right behind them, but as the two men raced into the room, they discovered that the boys were not there. It seemed the boys vanished into thin air! The workers immediately gathered up their tools, went back to the maintenance office where they explained to Harold what happened and said that was more than they expected and quit right there on the spot.

We were given permission to investigate the old hospital thanks to Bill and the owner of the hospital at the time, so on the evening of October 17, 2015, six members of Tri-C Ghost Hunters, including myself and one guest, Mari, entered St. Joseph Hospital. Mari was also instrumental in obtaining permission for us to do the investigation. We were the first team ever to investigate inside the hospital and were hoping we could validate others' paranormal claims and experiences. We split up into two teams and started exploring and investigating inside the building. Since this was our first time investigating this location, I had no idea where any of the active locations were, but I did know the stories Bill and Harold relayed to me. Two of the areas we concentrated on were the basement and the emergency room area. Both teams investigated for several hours with no activity when the excited voice of one of our investigators came over the walkie-talkie, "We saw the boy in the ER!" My team raced to the ER in hopes of seeing the boy too and to find out what happened. The ER is small compared to modern-day hospital emergency rooms. Along two opposite walls are where the patient beds used to be located and some areas still had the divider curtains hanging from rails on the ceiling. At one end of the room was the nurses' station and on each side of the nurses' station are two doors, one that leads to some offices and treatment rooms and the other leading into the radiology room. Once we were all in the ER, Jacky who saw the boy, said one investigator, Robin, was at the nurses' station and Mari was at the other end of the ER. Jacky was walking around the ER introducing herself as "Nurse Jacky." She began pulling the curtains back saying, "If anyone needs help, all you have to do is ask." At that moment, something out of the corner of her eye caught her attention. When she looked, she observed a young boy peeking his head around the door frame from the radiology room…the same room where the two workers previously

Photo 57 – Where the little "boy" was seen

had their encounter with the two young boys (photo 57). She went on to say he was laughing and pointing his finger at her. Not thinking, Jacky immediately ran toward him, yelling at the other team members that she saw the little boy. The ghostly boy turned and ran from the room in the same direction the other two had run. Jacky chased him down a hall and into the same room the other boys ran into. When Jacky ran into the room, the young boy had disappeared, as well. Jacky described the boy as being about eight years old with dark hair, wearing a checkered shirt and jean overalls. She stated he looked like a regular living boy, except for one thing…he was gray from head to toe, like he had just stepped out of an old black and white movie!

After Jacky told us what happened, all of us searched the ER area, including the offices, treatment rooms, old ER and the surrounding rooms for the boy, to no avail. He was nowhere to be found and never appeared again for the rest of the night, but we may have encountered him again the following month.

On November 7, 2015, we had our second investigation at St. Joseph Hospital. This time, 12 members of our team participated, enough to cover the majority of the hospital, but like the prior investigation, we concentrated on the basement and emergency room. This time we placed a teddy bear trigger object on the counter at the nurses' station in the ER. For those who may not know, a trigger object is an object that may prompt a response or action from a certain spirit in which contact is trying to be made. In this case, we used a teddy bear to attract a young child. This particular teddy bear also had a REM pod motion sensor built in. REM means Radiating Electro-Magneticity, which basically means if anything comes close to the bear or attempts to pick it up, an audible alarm will be triggered. My wife Kathy was sitting alone on the floor in the radiology room conducting an EVP session with an audio recorder and headphones, which enable the investigator to hear any possible EVPs in real time. No one else besides Kathy was in the radiology room or the emergency room. A little while into the session, Kathy heard through her headphones the voice of a young boy saying, "Thank you." Immediately afterwards, the alarm on the teddy bear went off, indicating that something was near the bear. Was the young boy happy that we brought him a teddy bear to play with? We may never know who this boy is or why he is still there, but we haven't given up hope.

Since those first two investigations, Tri-C Ghost Hunters has investigated the hospital numerous times over the past several years and many members have had frightening and unexplainable encounters, from apparitions standing alongside them and objects being thrown to countless doors being slammed and investigators being slapped and pushed. It has been a worthwhile endeavor as Tri-C Ghost Hunters also conducted numerous public events and private ghost hunts at the hospital with all of the money received from these events being donated to local charities. From January 2016 to the date of this publication, Tri-C Ghost Hunters has donated $28,126 to local charities. We have also raised and donated 1,720 pounds of food to the local food bank.

We have turned an old unwanted and abandoned building that was scheduled for demolition into hope for all of the residents of the City of Lorain and Lorain County, Ohio. That is one of the many reasons I enjoy doing what I do.

For further information on Tri-C Ghost Hunters please visit their website at www.tcghohio.org.

Note: Tri-C Ghost Hunters no longer conducts public or private events inside St. Joseph Hospital due to hazardous and unsafe conditions inside the building.

Chapter Eleven

PARANORMAL INVESTIGATIONS

TECHNIQUES OF THE INVESTIGATION

For centuries, mankind has been fascinated with ghosts and the afterlife. Nearly every ancient culture had their beliefs in an afterlife and that there was no doubt when someone died, their soul moved on to a different realm, the land of the dead if you will. Ghost stories of loved ones returning from the dead can be found in almost every past civilization, including those in Mesopotamia, Egypt, Greece, China, Rome, India and many others.

One of the earliest written accounts of a ghostly encounter that wasn't in the Bible was documented in the first century A.D., by the great Roman author and statesman Pliny the Younger[87] (61-c. 113). His written account centers on a haunted house in Rome inhabited by the ghost of an old, emaciated, bearded man wearing chains. Inhabitants of the house became so frightened by the nightly visitor that they could not stay there very long. Because of this, the house was constantly for sale or rent. A Roman philosopher named Athenodorus heard of the stories and decided to move in, immersing himself in his writings whenever the ghost would appear. He finally decided he could not ignore the ghostly spirit any longer and followed the apparition into the yard where it disappeared before his eyes. Athenodorus decided to have the ground dug up at the exact location where the spirit vanished. The corpse of a man wrapped in heavy chains was discovered buried at that exact location. From that day forward, the spirit was never seen or heard from again.

As you can see, there have been reports of ghosts for centuries and since the invention of the camera and other electronic equipment, people have been trying to capture proof of their existence. The problem at present is there has been no scientific proof that ghosts or the afterlife exist. Sure, there are countless photographs and video recordings of alleged ghosts and hauntings, but none of them were captured using scientific methods. Many investigators claim they use scientific equipment, therefore their investigation and any evidence captured was scientific in nature. This is a misconception among investigators. To conduct a scientific investigation, you should use the Scientific Method as defined in the "Merriam-Webster Dictionary" as *"principles and procedures for the systematic pursuit of knowledge involving the recognition and formulation of a problem, the collection of data through observation and experiment, and the formulation and testing of hypotheses."*[88] I do not want to get into the details and workings of the scientific method, for this chapter is focused on the basics of a paranormal investigation. I can, however, recommend a book for further reading on this method, *The Art and Science of Paranormal Investigation* by Jeffrey Dwyer, Ph.D.[89]

There are countless in-depth books on how to conduct a paranormal investigation and this chapter is not attempting to be one of those books. There are numerous ways to investigate and I am not telling anyone the right or wrong way to investigate. I am going to tell you how I conduct my investigations, which by the way, I do not claim to be scientific. When I conducted my first investigation in 1991 (Insights into the Unknown: A Ghost Hunter's Journey – Chapter Two, My First Investigation), I did it for the excitement of possibly capturing a ghost or other poltergeist activity. I was not trying to prove anything to anyone; I just wanted to prove to myself that these things existed. Since 2005, I now conduct investigations to try to help people figure out what is happening in their homes or businesses. Some of these people believe their homes or businesses are haunted by negative spirits and/or demons, which in my experience, is rarely, if ever, the reason. At the time of this publication, I have been involved in 250-300 investigations and have never, ever come upon anything demonic. I am not saying it doesn't happen, but only that those are extreme, rare cases.

You don't need a lot of equipment to investigate, but whatever equipment you do use, please make sure you know how to use it and its limitations. The majority of the equipment paranormal investigators use was not developed for paranormal research, but other applications. Paranormal investigators and enthusiasts have adapted those pieces of equipment for investigations based on theory.

There are two main types of hauntings, as well as several types of locations to investigate. The two main types of hauntings are intelligent and residual. An intelligent haunting is one in which any ghosts or spirits that are present will interact with you. They will answer questions or do something you request of them, such as closing that door or turning on that light. In a residual haunting there are no intelligent ghosts or spirits present and no interaction. It is more like a tape recorder that under certain conditions will play a past event over and over. There are different types of haunted locations you can investigate divided into outdoor locations such as cemeteries and battlefields and indoor locations. You can also divide indoor locations into known public locations such as the Ohio State Reformatory in Mansfield, Ohio, and the Trans-Allegheny Lunatic Asylum in Weston, West Virginia, and unknown locations such as a private home or business. The difference between these indoor locations is places like the Ohio State Reformatory already have a well-known history and documented paranormal activity, where on the other hand, private locations do not.

I will only be talking about indoor private homes and business investigations, but you can adapt some of these to the other types of locations, as well. One thing you want to keep in mind, though, is to not enter the process believing that the home or business is haunted. Go into the investigation with a skeptical mind and find logical explanations first and, above all, use COMMON SENSE.

INITIAL CONTACT AND INTERVIEW

After a request is made for help, the first thing I do is to conduct an interview with the client. I always like to make my initial contact and interview over the phone. The majority of requests I receive are by email through our Tri-C Ghost Hunters website. I may respond to the initial request by an email, but I always follow that up with a phone call. There is too great of a chance of my email going into their spam folder, which is not a good thing when people are reaching out to you for help. The ideal interview should be conducted face to face, but that isn't always possible, especially if the clients live some distance away. If the clients live closer, you can meet with them to conduct what I call a pre-investigation and to do another more in-depth interview. The bottom line is your initial contact should be done by phone, not email or text, for that matter.

The interview is one of the most important aspects of an investigation and can set the stage for a proper investigation. It can also give you some insight into the clients' psyche to see if they are sincere and possibly frightened, are making things up for attention or have a mental disorder. Be very careful on the latter. You don't want to tell someone they are crazy or mental, but be aware you may be talking with an elderly client who has dementia…I know, it has happened to me. Kathy and I conducted a pre-investigation one time at a private home in Northeast Ohio. Our client, who was elderly, was talking about things that didn't make sense or instances with logical explanations, such as bees in the basement and "different" trash on the tree lawn for trash day. She was so frightened that her home was taken over by demons that she put her house up for sale. Luckily there was a family member there who agreed that there was possibly something mentally wrong with her and was going to get her the help she needed. I have even been on private home investigations where the clients treated the investigation as a party, complete with family, friends and alcohol. Needless to say, those investigations are over before they even start. Based on the answers I receive to my questions, I can determine if the clients need a pre-investigation, full investigation or no investigation at all. Most of the time, the clients are very sincere and believe that their home or business is indeed haunted, which at least warrants a pre-investigation if they are close enough. I will get into the difference between a pre-investigation and a full investigation further on in this chapter. Please see Appendix II for a sample questionnaire that Tri-C Ghost Hunters uses for our interviews. Feel free to use this questionnaire and make changes as you see fit.

RESEARCH

The next thing to do is research on the address, city, area and occupants. There are numerous resources for your research, including the internet, newspapers, libraries, historical societies, county property records and local law enforcement agencies. Try to find out as much as you can about the house and the land it was built on. Learn who the past owners were and what the land was historically used for. Maybe there was a Native American village or an old family cemetery that was moved. Also take into consideration the land the property sits on goes back thousands and thousands of years prior to the arrival of Europeans. Police reports, which are public record, can give you information on any crimes that may have occurred in recent years at the house or business you will be investigating. Police reports can also give you information on any people residing there. Just as it is important to protect your clients, it is just as important, if not more, to protect your team and yourself. You don't want to be walking into an unstable household or situation. Please be tactful when reaching out to police departments, newspapers and such. Please don't say, "I am doing research at such and such an address because they believe their home is haunted." Keep the reason for the research confidential. Another good resource is neighbors, especially ones who have lived in the neighborhood a number of years, but be careful, especially if your clients want their case to remain confidential. Remember this very important point…your clients' privacy is of utmost importance! If you have permission from your clients, then go talk with neighbors. They may know important information about past owners or any other pertinent information that can help you in your investigation. I like to have as much information as I can prior to an investigation. I know some investigators do not, and like going in cold, but this is not a game, at least not for me. Someone needs help and the more information I have, the more I may be able to help them. Understand, though, that your research may not uncover any reasons why the location may be haunted. There may have been no murders, suicides, deaths or other traumatic events that occurred on the property. There could be other reasons such as ghosts or spirits passing through or deceased loved ones keeping a watch over family members. I have investigated several cases where these were the causes of activity taking place in the home or business.

PRE-INVESTIGATION AND INVESTIGATION

My team does two types of investigations: pre-investigations and investigations. A pre-investigation is a very short tour/investigation of the home or business that lasts about 1-2 hours. We do a pre-investigation if we are not sure the location warrants a larger investigation. Sometimes we can determine this while doing the phone interview. If the client is telling you they get strange feelings of being watched while in their bedroom or every once in a while, a light will turn off by itself, then this would only warrant a pre-investigation. If they tell you everyone in the household is experiencing things such as doors opening and closing, voices, frightened pets and apparitions, then this would definitely warrant a full-blown investigation. You have to take each client on a case-by-case basis if they warrant a full investigation or not.

When we do a pre-investigation, we go in with a smaller team of 2-4 investigators. We ask the client for a tour of the premises, paying close attention to where any activity has taken place. After the tour, one member will then hold a more in-depth interview with the client and any others who reside inside the home, while the other investigator(s) inspect the home for any logical explanations. Equipment we use is limited to an audio recorder, which we have recording the whole time, a camera, carbon monoxide detector and EMF detectors. EMF detectors are very important during a pre-investigation as they can determine high EMF in certain areas of the home. We do not use EMF detectors to locate ghosts or spirits during a pre-investigation, but to locate man-made electrical fields. See section on EMF detectors later in this chapter for additional information. One case in which we conducted a pre-investigation involved a carbon monoxide leak in the basement. Our client stated she didn't like the basement or the kitchen and always had funny feelings in both locations. During our pre-investigation, we discovered a carbon monoxide leak in the basement through the use of our carbon monoxide detector. We immediately got everyone out of the home and called the gas company. Once the gas company arrived, the technician discovered a large gas leak coming from the furnace in the basement, as well as a smaller gas leak coming from the gas stove in the kitchen. He advised us if we did not discover the leaks, they could have killed all of the occupants. So, as you can see, conducting a pre-investigation can save you time and possibly save someone's life.

A full investigation is warranted when it is not possible to do a pre-investigation or when you believe something paranormal, based on your interview, is occurring in the home or business. When Tri-C Ghost Hunters conducts a full investigation, we bring all of our equipment plus a few more investigators. Depending on the size of the location, we may have 4-6 investigators. Another important factor to consider is the number of people living in the home. You want to try to have as few household members during the investigation as possible. If someone seems to be a "trigger" object, it may be wise to have that person involved in the investigation. If it is a young child, you may not want them present during the investigation. We always ask the parents to not have any children present during the investigation, but that decision is clearly up to them. Another distraction during an investigation is pets. You don't want cats and dogs wandering around the premises as you are trying to conduct your investigation because contamination of any audio and video recordings will definitely occur. See if the clients can have all the pets removed from the home. This is sometimes easier said than done. Just remind the clients that to do a proper investigation, it is best not to have any cats or dogs present. We have even done investigations where the pets stayed with us in the base of operations. A real problem pet is any type of bird. We conducted one investigation where the client had about four or five large parrots. Needless to say, they talked and squawked throughout the investigation and were so loud and noisy that we had to cut the investigation short.

Once we arrive at the location, just like for a pre-investigation, we will ask for a tour of the premises, paying close attention to all of the "hot spots," the locations where most of the activity is reported. We always have at least one audio recorder going during the tour. Better yet, it is a good idea to record the tour with a video camera. During the tour you can also determine the best location for your base of operations. A base of operations is a location preferably outside of the house or business such as a garage or shed, where the DVR (digital video recorder) monitor can be set up. It is also used as a place to store extra equipment and where members and clients can stay during the duration of the investigation when not actually investigating. After our tour, everyone on the team will have a job to do. Some will start setting up equipment, others will log temperature and EMF readings in each room of the location and still another will draw a diagram of the whole premises to indicate the temperature and EMF readings. The diagram will also show where each piece of equipment is located, including DVR cameras. Another good practice upon arrival is to log the date, time and weather and atmospheric conditions, such as outdoor temperatures, wind, humidity, rain, snow, barometric pressure, dew point, UV index and air quality. Other good information to obtain is space weather, such as moon phases, geometric storms and solar flares. It is also good practice to check and log the weather information again after completing the investigation. All of this gathered data may not reveal any useful information at the time, but compared to other investigations you do, you may find a correlation on any activity encountered and the weather and space conditions at the time.

Once we complete our tour, setup and data gathering, some team members may say prayers of protection. If that is something you feel is important, by all means, do whatever protection ritual/prayer you feel comfortable with.

It is now time to begin the actual investigation. We like breaking up into small teams of no more than two investigators. While one team is inside the home or business investigating, the other team(s) will be at base with the clients watching the DVR monitor for anything unusual and logging the same. If a client wants to participate in the investigation, that is okay -- it is their home or business. They would just have to be taught the etiquettes of participating in the investigation, such as being quiet during certain portions of the investigation. Each team will take turns investigating for a predetermined amount of time, unless they are experiencing activity, then they will continue a little longer. Again, there is no right or wrong way -- this is just the way we do it. Obviously, if there are only a couple of you, investigate the whole time with some breaks. For any investigation, I would not recommend investigating alone for a couple of reasons. First, if there is activity, you have another witness and second, and most importantly, safety. You don't have to worry too much about safety when conducting a private home investigation, but at other darker and larger locations, there can be a greater risk of personal injury with no one around to lend assistance.

There is no set length to an investigation and it doesn't have to be dark either. You can investigate during the day or with the lights on -- it does not matter -- paranormal activity happens around the clock. In a smaller place without much activity, you may only be there 4-6 hours. Other larger locations may warrant eight to 10 hours or even longer. Most paranormal activity doesn't happen on cue. Sometimes a person reporting activity may only experience it a few times a month at different times and days of the week, so trying to capture any evidence of paranormal activity is like trying to find a needle in a haystack. Sometimes you get lucky and other times you don't.

If you do hear or see something unusual during your investigation, don't assume it is paranormal. Be logical and try to figure out and recreate what you just heard or saw. Remember -- not everything you hear and see is paranormal.

Once the investigation is over, it is time to pack up all of your equipment and any note/logs you may have.

If you said a prayer of protection or some other ritual at the start of the investigation, it is also a good idea to say a closing prayer or ritual at the end of the investigation so nothing negative attaches itself to you or follows you home.

FOLLOW-UP/REVEAL

Now comes the fun part -- reviewing all of your audio and video! This is a very time-consuming and tedious process. I have sat for hours and hours listening to audio and watching video. You have to be very attentive and alert when reviewing your evidence less you miss something important. Even though it is very monotonous, it can also be very worthwhile, especially when you capture that awesome EVP (Electronic Voice Phenomenon) or something unexplainable on video.

After everyone on the team is finished reviewing their evidence, it will be compiled and entered into a written report for our clients. Depending on where they live, we will mail the report to them with any evidence captured or we will meet with them personally to go over the investigation. If there is evidence, we will allow them to listen to or watch it and then give them their own copies.

I like to keep in contact with our clients after the investigation to see if they are continuing to experience any further activity and to conduct additional investigations, if necessary.

Now let's discuss some paranormal equipment you can use during an investigation. There are four main pieces of equipment I like to use: cameras, video cameras, audio recorders and EMF detectors.

CAMERAS

Cameras are an important part of any investigation. I mostly use a camera to document a location and not necessarily to capture evidence. In my opinion, capturing any type of paranormal evidence on a camera is extremely rare. During my past investigations, I have taken roughly 25,000-30,000 photographs and out of that amount, I only have 12 that I would consider possibly paranormal in nature. That is only .048% - .040%, which means you would have to take around 2,500 photographs before you captured anything that could be considered paranormal.

There are all types of cameras on the market, including film, compact digital, digital SLR, mirrorless, 360 and smartphones, just to name a few. All of them are great for taking photographs and it doesn't matter if it's film or digital or even how many megapixels a camera has, but there is one camera I would never use during an investigation and that is a smartphone camera. Smartphones are fantastic and convenient for taking photographs of your cousin's wedding, your vacation or your grandchildren, but are awful and unreliable for use during a paranormal investigation. They are notorious for creating false anomalies due to the size of the lens, shutter speed and zoom, which creates motion blur and low-quality photographs, especially in low-light conditions, not to mention there are some smartphone apps that claim to take photos of ghosts...really! With smartphone apps you can also add ghostly mists, shadows and apparitions to your photos very easily. Using a smartphone camera during an investigation is like using a Swiss army knife when you really need a decent hunting knife. All of the gadgets and apps are pretty cool, but it just won't get the job done right.

The difference between using a film camera and a digital camera is a digital camera will show you immediate pictures of the photographs you just took, which are great for trying to debunk a questionable photo. With film cameras, you have no idea if you captured anything unusual until you have the film developed, but because there is a negative, it will be very difficult to manipulate a photograph into something it is not. Photographs taken with digital cameras are very easy to manipulate and change, one reason I am always very skeptical when someone sends me a photograph asking for my opinion. However, there are digital image forensic websites available where you can submit a photograph to find out everything about that photo, including the brand and model of the camera, date and time photo was taken, file type, metadata information and if the photograph was used in any software program, such as Photoshop.

One other item you have to be aware of when taking photographs is the phenomenon of orbs. Orbs are round balls of light, varying in size, usually white, but can be any color consisting of concentric circles. The majority of orbs are white, but others could be red, blue, gold, green or any other color. Some people see faces inside the orbs and many people believe orbs to be angels, ghosts or the spirits of the loved ones coming back to visit. There is no evidence whatsoever to indicate that orbs are spirit energy. I personally do not believe orbs are paranormal in nature and here is why. The first digital cameras marketed for consumers came out in the late 1990s and shortly thereafter people started seeing balls of light in their photographs, especially in outdoor locations such as cemeteries and low-light or dark conditions like you would have during a paranormal investigation. When Kathy and I first started investigating together, we did think orbs were spirits, but that changed when we started experimenting with cameras and orbs. Because of our experiments, there is no doubt in our minds that orbs are nothing more than dust, bugs, pollen, moisture and rain. I will not go into details into the internal workings of a digital camera and why it captures orbs for there are many websites on the internet that can explain this phenomenon in more detail. There are orbs related to paranormal activity, but those you will be able to see with your naked eye. Kathy saw a true orb during one of our investigations. She was walking past a stairway, when she observed a white ball of light floating down the stairs, disappearing when it got to the bottom.

Other types of cameras you can use during an investigation are FLIR cameras (Forward-looking infrared) also known as thermal imaging cameras and trail cams. A FLIR camera is a thermographic camera that senses infrared radiation. A trail camera, also known as a game camera or remote camera, is a stationary camera that can record photographs and video triggered by motion.

One thing to remember during an investigation is to take as many photographs as you can. You never know what you may capture.

VIDEO CAMERAS

There are many different types of consumer video cameras, both old and new. When I conducted my first investigation in 1991, I used an RCA VHS video camera that you had to rest on your shoulder and look through an eyepiece while you videotaped -- not good when you are walking around a dark location that you're not familiar with! They were also not equipped with consumer night vision until around 1998 when Sony introduced their Night Shot. The only good thing about VHS tapes at the time was they could record for a maximum of six hours before the tape had to be changed. After VHS, I moved on to Hi8 and Mini-DV camcorders. They were smaller than the VHS camcorders, but the recording time was only about two hours for the Hi8 and 90 minutes for the Mini-DV, which meant on a stationary camera, you had to return every hour and a half to change the tape, which was very inconvenient. Another downfall concerning the Hi8 and Mini-DV is you had to keep purchasing tapes because it was wise to use a brand-new tape for each investigation. You should never use an old tape to record a new investigation. The nice thing about these two types of cameras, however, is their size, which is smaller than the old VHS cameras. You can still purchase both of these types of cameras online, as well as the cassette tapes.

In this day and age of the digital revolution, I now use a camcorder with a built-in hard drive. These types of cameras are really convenient as there are no tapes to purchase and change and the recording times can last for hours and hours depending on the size of the hard drive. Other types of video cameras include the GoPro and DVR systems. Whichever video camera you decide to use, make sure you set them up as stationary cameras in areas where activity has taken place and to have at least one video camera with you recording at all times. I use either a GoPro attached to a chest harness or carry a digital video camera on a tripod and place it in a strategic area of each room I investigate. Please make sure you also have a good external IR (infrared) light with each of your video cameras.

One last tip: video cameras also pick up orbs flying around, so please be aware of that.

AUDIO RECORDERS

Besides your senses, an audio recorder is the most important type of equipment you can have during an investigation. The vast majority of evidence captured are EVPs, known as Electronic Voice Phenomenon. Don't get EVPs confused with disembodied voices. EVPs cannot be heard at the time; wherein disembodied voices can be heard. EVPs are nothing new in the paranormal field. One of the greatest inventors of our time, Thomas Edison, announced in 1920 that one day it would be possible to communicate with the dead and that he was working on a "spirit phone" to accomplish just that. Unfortunately, he was never able to produce a phone or any other device to speak with the dead prior to his death in 1931[90].

One of the first EVPs ever recorded happened by accident in 1959 by Friedrich Jurgenson[91]. Jurgenson was a man of all trades -- he was a philosopher, painter, archeologist, singer and film maker. One day, he was using a tape recorder to record bird songs in the forest. When he played the tape back, he heard human voices on the recording, even though he was alone in the forest. He became so intrigued by these voices from beyond the grave that he continued making recordings in attempts to capture more voices. In 1964, he published a book about his EVP experiences titled "*Rosterna fran Rymden*" (Voices from Space)[92].

Any type of audio recording device will do when attempting to record EVPs. Jurgenson recorded his EVPs on old reel-to-reel tape recorders. You can use reel-to-reel, cassette recorder, digital recorder, smartphone audio recording apps, video camera and any other device that can record audio. Some are worse than others though, such as the cassette recorder. A cassette recorder will record the whirring of the internal mechanisms, which can potentially interfere with any recordings, so be aware of that.

There are three basic classifications of EVPs: Class A, B and C. Class A is the best, with the voices clear and understandable. Class B voices are a little more difficult. People hear voices and words, but not everyone agrees on what is being said. Class C are the most difficult to understand. You believe there is a voice, but cannot make out what is being said. I never use a Class C EVP as evidence since nothing is really clear.

One interesting thing I have discovered about the EVPs I have recorded is all of them are no longer than three words in length. Examples are "How's it going?", "They already left," "It's okay," "Help me," "I don't mind" and "I did," just to name a few. I have never recorded any EVPs longer than that, though I have heard about other EVPs recorded by other investigators that are longer, sometimes making complete sentences, but I believe those are rare.

Here are some general guidelines to follow when trying to record EVPs and what I have found that works for me:

1) Be aware of your surroundings. Human voices can carry, especially at night. You may be in one part of a building and other investigators may be in another part. Just because you are separated from the others doesn't mean you won't pick up their talking on your

recorder. Beware of vents and ductwork too. Voices can travel through those also.

2) At the beginning of an EVP session we always state the date, time, location and area inside that location. We also have everyone present introduce themselves. We do the introductions for a couple of reasons. When you are reviewing the audio at a later date, you know how many people were present during the session, as well as what each person sounds like on audio. It is also a friendly gesture for any ghosts or spirits that may be present.

3) When doing an EVP session with others, please talk in a normal voice. Under no circumstances should anyone be whispering. It is too difficult to remember who was whispering at different times during the recording. If you have something to say, just say it in a normal voice. If someone does whisper, make sure you call it out to mark it on your recording.

4) Call out any unusual sounds you hear, including other people talking both inside and outside a location. Other noises you will hear during an EVP session are outside noises such as animal sounds, air and automobile traffic; weather conditions such as wind, rain, hail and thunder and bodily functions such as belching, stomach growling, sighs, ahhs, yawns, bones/joints cracking, sniffles, sneezes, hiccups and flatulence.

5) Keep movement to a minimum and if you have to get up and walk around or you have to change your position while seated, make sure you call it out.

6) It is always a good idea to have a least two audio recorders recording at the same time so that you can cross-reference any possible EVPs you may have recorded.

7) In my experience, the majority of EVPs I have recorded is when no direct questions are asked. Try not to ask these general types of questions: What is your name? Did you die here? What did you die of? Why are you still here? Instead just have a conversation among the investigators present. Talk about the location and its history. Try playing music that could be associated with the location as a trigger object. For example, if you are investigating in Gettysburg, try playing music from the Civil War, especially Union and Confederate marching songs. You may be surprised at the number of EVPs you may record. Remember, Jurgenson wasn't trying to make contact by asking any questions -- he was just recording bird songs.

8) It is always a good idea to review your audio using a good pair of over-the-ear headphones and an audio editing program such as Audacity, Ocenaudio and WavePad just to name a few. These and other audio editing programs can be downloaded for free from the internet. Using these types of programs will allow you to "clean up" your audio to be able to determine what the EVP is actually saying.

EMF DETECTORS

Pretty much everything today emits some level of EMF (Electro-Magnetic Field), but high EMF in a specific location, sometimes called a "fear cage," can cause people to experience nausea, headaches, paranoia and hallucination, among other psychical conditions. It is still unclear if a continuous exposure to high EMF can cause serious physical ailments such as cancer, but studies are ongoing. There are two main types of EMF: those that are man-made such as EMF that is emitted through microwaves, televisions, cellular phones and anything electrical; and natural EMF that is emitted through the sun, thunderstorms and the earth's core.

Understanding and knowing how EMF is transmitted is extremely important during a paranormal investigation. High man-made or natural EMF in a home or business can cause the owners, residents and employees to believe the location is haunted. In our brains are nerve cells called neurons, a cell that receives, processes and transmits information throughout the brain and body by electrical and chemical signals. Exposure to high EMF can affect this process.

When I investigate, one of the first things I do is conduct a sweep of the home or business to search for man-made EMF with the use of EMF detectors, such as a K-II meter, Cell Sensor or Mel-meter. All of these devices are capable of finding EMF in a location through audible signals, lights and digital/needle readings. There are other EMF detectors on the market, but those are the three I use. I also use a Tri-Field Natural meter to search for natural EMF in a location.

Sometimes we find no high EMF in a home or business and other times we have discovered extremely high concentrations of EMF that have contributed to the residents believing their home was haunted. One particular pre-investigation my wife Kathy and I conducted was a private home in Middleburg Heights, Ohio. The homeowners contacted us and stated they needed help because they believed their home was haunted, especially the master bedroom. Upon our arrival at the home, the clients relayed that strange things were going on they couldn't explain, with most of them occurring in the master bedroom. Both of them stated they would have strange feelings while in the bedroom, like they were being watched and their personalities would change, always leading to arguments. Kathy and I entered the bedroom and we could feel the energy right away and suspected it was probably not paranormal in nature. We took our Mel-meter and started checking for high EMF in the room. It didn't take us long to figure out what was going on. The ceiling fan, which was directly above the bed, registered a reading of 23.4 milligauss. A clock radio on the nightstand next to the bed had a reading of 34.5 milligauss. Many experts believe continued exposure to anything over 2.0 milligauss is harmful. To make matters worse, the bedroom was right above the master electrical panel in the basement that was also emitting high EMF. This was a classic "fear cage" with high EMF permeating the bedroom. We advised them the root of all of their problems was the ceiling fan, clock radio and the electrical panel in the basement and once they correct those issues, all their problems should go away.

EMF activity in an area can indicate possible paranormal activity as many paranormal investigators and enthusiasts theorize that ghosts and spirits are detectable energy that can be identified through EMF "hits." However, there is no proof to back up this theory. Investigators counter that if there was no EMF detected in a certain area at the beginning of an investigation and later there is EMF detected in that same area, it must be paranormal. That could be possible, but know this, man-made devices such as cell phones (phone calls, text messages, notifications), communication towers and emergency radio frequencies such as police, fire and rescue can set off EMF detectors. It may be good practice to turn off your cell phones during an investigation or, better yet, leave them at base turned off and make note of any communication towers and police, fire and hospital locations nearby.

Remember this important point...not everything is paranormal and what a lot of people experience can be attributed to high EMF.

OTHER TYPES OF EQUIPMENT

Digital cameras, video cameras, audio recorders and EMF detectors should be on every paranormal investigator equipment list, but there is a wide variety of other equipment that can be used for paranormal investigations. There is no right or wrong way to investigate and there are no wrong pieces of equipment either when it comes to investigating the paranormal. You just have to know how each piece of equipment works and its shortcomings.

Other pieces of equipment I have used during my investigations include:

- ITC (Instrumental Trans Communication) devices -- ghost box/ghost portal
- Spirit Boxes (SB-7 & SB-11)
- Motion Detectors
- Proximity Detectors
- REM Pods
- EM Pumps
- Thermometers
- Compasses
- Geo-Phones
- Baby Monitors
- Parascope 360s
- SLS Connect Cameras
- Carbon Monoxide Detectors
- Dowsing Rods
- Pendulums
- Flashlights

RIDDING HOMES OF GHOSTS

A lot of people ask us how to get rid of ghosts or spirits. Some of our clients don't want to get rid of them. They feel comfortable knowing they are there, but others want them removed. The bottom line is we cannot guarantee that any type of ghost or spirit will leave. We do have investigators and psychics on our team who can sage and clear homes. Sometimes we will advise our clients to contact the clergy from their church to bless the house. There is one thing that we tell our clients to do that seems to work, which is "Take back your home." Walk around your home and say in a loud, stern voice, in every room, that this is my house and you are not welcome here and tell them to leave now! They may have to do it several times. It seems simple, but it has worked. This would not work for a home where there are demonic entities, but like I said earlier, those are very rare and extreme cases. It would also not work for a residual haunting since there would be no intelligent entity present.

Our goal is to make our clients feel safe and comfortable in their homes and businesses and we will do everything in our power to accomplish that goal.

I have shown you how I conduct my investigations and the four main pieces of equipment I like to use. Take what I have shown you and adopt what you like into your investigations. I will close with this: enjoy what you do, do it for the right reasons, use your common sense, think outside the box and, above all, be safe on your journey down those roads into the unknown.

Appendix I

AFTERLIFE - Life after our physical body dies.

AGENT - A living person who is the focus of poltergeist activity. Typically, a teenage female.

ANGEL - Messengers of God who can also protect and guide human beings.

ANNIVERSARY IMPRINT - An imprint that usually manifests around the same time each year.

ANOMALY - Something that is out of place and unexplained.

APPARITION - A disembodied soul or spirit that can be seen visually.

APPORT - A physical object that can materialize and appear at will, and can include coins, watches, jewelry and even food.

ARTEFACT - Term used to describe the slight noises or residual images produced by the internal mechanisms of equipment which could be misinterpreted as paranormal sounds or images.

ASTRAL BODY - The body that a person occupies during an out-of-body experience.

ASTRAL PLANE - A world that is believed to exist above our physical world.

ASTRAL PROJECTION - The conscious initiation of an out-of-body experience.

AUDIO VOICE PHENOMENON (AVP) - Disembodied voices that are heard at the time of the investigation, and may or may not be recorded on electronic devices.

AURA - A field of energy that emanates from matter. It is especially prominent around living things.

AUTOMATIC WRITING - A method used by spirit mediums to obtain information from the "other side."

BANISHING - Procedure to cast a paranormal entity from a location.

BANSHEE - A death omen or spirit that attaches itself to certain families.

BENIGN SPIRIT - A spirit that is harmless or has no ill intentions.

BILOCATION - A phenomenon where a person seems to be at more than one location at the same time. (See doppelganger)

CHANNELING - In this method of spirit communication a spirit will pass information directly to a medium or channeler who will then relay the information to others.

CLAIRAUDIENCE - Hearing voices, astral music or discarnate beings.

CLAIREOFACTOR - To have an extraordinary sense of smell, as if you could smell flowers before they bloom or smell trouble before it happens or death before it occurs.

CLAIRSENTIENCE - The ability to clearly feel yours and/or another's emotions and sensations.

CLAIRVOYENCE - The ability to obtain knowledge based on unexplainable intuition, vision or psychic senses.

CLEARING - Ridding a location of ghostly activity.

COLD SPOTS - Patches of cool/cold air strewn about haunted locations.

COLLECTIVE APPARITION - A type of ghost sighting that occurs when one or more people see the same apparition.

CRISIS APPARITION - An apparition that is seen when a person is seriously ill, seriously injured or at the point of death.

DEBUNK - To show or prove something as false.

DEMATERIALIZATION - The sudden disappearance of a person or spirit in full view of witnesses.

DEMON - Fallen angels under the command of Satan.

DEMONOLOGIST - One who studies and practices the art of demonology. An individual who specializes in the removal of evil or demonic forces from a given environment using the art of demonology.

DEMONOLOGY - The study of demons or beliefs about demons.

DIRECT WRITING - Where spirits actually communicate by the use of writing.

DISEMBODIED - Having no physical body.

DISEMBODIED VOICE - A voice that is heard with human ears whose source comes from someone without a physical body.

DIVINING/DOWSING RODS - A forked rod from a tree said to indicate the presence of water or minerals underground. May also indicate an energy field. Can also be made of metal.

DOPPELGANGER - A ghost of the present that looks identical to a living person, but behaves differently.

DOUBLE - A ghost of the present that looks identical to a living person, and behaves identically.

DIVINATION/DOWSING - Interpreting the motions of rods, sticks, pendulums, and other such instruments to obtain information (also called diving).

DIRECT VOICE PHENOMENON (DVP) - An auditory "spirit" voice that is spoken directly to the sitter's at a séance.

EARTHBOUND - Refers to a ghost that is unable to cross over at the time of death.

ECTOPLASM - A substance that allegedly oozes from ghosts or spirits and makes it possible for them to materialize, and perform feats of telekinesis.

ELECTRO-MAGNETIC FIELD (EMF) - A physical field produced by electrically charged objects. It affects the behavior of charged objects in the vicinity of the field.

ELECTRONIC VOICE PHENOMENON (EVP) - Disembodied voices or sounds that are captured on recording (audio or video) devices.

ELEMENTALS - A term used to describe angry or malicious spirits. Also known as "earth spirits."

EMF DETECTOR - An instrument for measuring the magnitude and direction of a magnetic field. Typically used by paranormal researchers to detect a ghost's magnetic energy.

ENTITY - A conscious, interactive ghost. Any being, including people and ghosts.

EXTRASENSORY PERCEPTION (ESP) - The knowledge of external objects or events without the aid of senses.

EXORCISM - The act of ridding a person or a location of demons/evil spirits by using religious rites.

EXORCIST - A person who performs the ridding of demons or other supernatural beings who are alleged to have possessed a person, or (sometimes) a building or even an object.

FALSE AWAKENING - Event in which a person believes they are awake but are actually dreaming.

FEAR CAGE - An area of high EMF readings which can bring out feelings of uneasiness, anxiety, and fear.

GAUSS - Is the centimeter-gram-second (CGS) of a magnetic field, which is also known as the "magnetic flux density" or the "magnetic induction."

GHOST - The soul of a deceased person or animal that can appear in visible form or other manifestations to the living. They have not gone through the light, and are stuck between the physical world and the afterlife.

GHOST BOX - A 2-way communication device used for communicating with spirits/ghosts.

GHOST HUNTER - One who seeks to experience, and document paranormal activity.

GHOST LIGHTS - Strange balls of light that appear in specific locations, often for an extended period of time.

GHOUL - Demonic or parasitic entity that feeds on human remains.

HALLUCINATION - Vivid perception of sights and/or sounds that are not physically present. Usually associated with an altered state of consciousness induced by alcohol, drugs, illness or psychological instability.

HARBINGER - A ghost of the future that brings warnings of impending events.

HAUNTING - Repeated manifestations of unexplained phenomenon that occur at a particular location.

HELLHOUND - Spectral death omen in the form of a ghostly dog.

HOT SPOT - An area within a haunted location where the activity is prominent and/or energy fields are focused.

ILLUSION - A perception between what is perceived, and what is reality.

IMPRINT - Events, energy, and strong feelings or emotions that are left on an object, a location or even a specific person.

INCUBUS - A demon in male form who, according to a number of mythological, and legendary traditions, lies upon sleepers, especially women, in order to have sex with them.

INFESTATION - See Possession.

INSTRUMENTAL TRANS-COMMUNICATION (ITC) - ITC is simply the use of modern electronic devices in an attempt to communicate with spirits. Can be attempted on radios, televisions, computers, telephones, and audio recorders.

INTELLIGENT HAUNTING - A haunting by an intelligent or conscious spirit which interacts with living persons.

INVESTIGATION - Carefully controlled research project in which various methods, and equipment are used to seek confirmation of reports of ghosts and hauntings.

LEVITATION - To lift or raise a physical object in apparent defiance of gravity.

LIVING APPARITION - The manifestation of an image of a living person that appears in a different location.

LUCID DREAM - A dream in which one is aware they are dreaming.

MALEVOLENT SPIRIT - A spirit who has ill intent.

MANIFESTATION - See Possession.

MATERIALIZATION - The act of forming something solid from air.

MATRIXING - The phenomenon of the mind to complete a picture that is not there.
MEDIUM - A person with the gift of communicating with the dead.

METAPHYSICS - The field of study of phenomenon that is best described as being beyond the laws of physics.

MILLIGAUSS - One thousandth of a gauss.

NATURAL - A rare phenomenon that appears ghostly but in fact is created by some scientifically unknown property of the present nature.

NEAR DEATH EXPERIENCE - Experiences of people that have been pronounced medically dead or very close to death.

NECROMANCY - Interacting with the dead, particularly for the purpose of communication or resurrection.

NEGATIVE ENTITY - Inhuman entity, demonic in nature.

NONHUMAN ENTITY - An entity that was never a human on earth. Consists of angels and demons.

OLD HAG SYNDROME - A sleep phenomena that involves a feeling of immobilization, suffocation, odd smells, and feelings, and is sometimes accompanied by immense fear.

OPPRESSION - See Possession.

ORBS - Round "lights" caught on film (still or video) that are believed by some to be related to paranormal activity. Very controversial. Most appear to be dust, bugs or moisture.

OUIJA BOARD - A flat board marked with letters of the alphabet, the numbers 0-9, the words yes, no, and goodbye. The Ouija board can supposedly be used to communicate with spirits of the dead. NOTE: IT IS BELIEVED BY SOME THAT IT CAN UNKNOWNINGLY INVITE DEMONS/EVIL SPIRITS INTO THE HOME.

OUT-OF-BODY EXPERIENCE - When one's consciousness exits the restrictions of the physical body.

PARANORMAL - Anything beyond what is normal.

PARANORMAL RESEARCH - The study of phenomenon currently considered unexplainable by mainstream sciences.

PARAPSYCHOLOGY - The study of mental abilities, and effects outside the usual realm of psychology. Parapsychology includes the study of ESP, ghosts, luck, psycho kinesis, and other paranormal phenomena.

PAREIDOLIA - The phenomenon when faces and /or shapes are often reported in objects such as doors, trees, clouds, bushes, food, and even animals. This is usually nothing paranormal. It is a trick of the mind.

PENDULUM - A small weight at the end of a cord or chain that is usually about six to ten inches long. The movement of the weight, when uninfluenced by other factors, can be used to detect areas of paranormal energy.

PHANTOM - Another name for a ghost or spirit. Many use the term to refer to ghosts that have been seen wearing robes or cloaks.

POLTERGEIST - German for "noisy ghost", usually associated with knocking or movement of objects, which usually involves an agent.

PORTAL - A theoretical doorway of energy, through which spirits may be able to enter or exit a location.

PORTENT - Something that foreshadows a coming event; omen, sign.

POSSESSION - The entry of a spirit into the body of a willing or unwilling host, in which the spirit takes control of the individual's motor and cognitive functions. There are anywhere from three to five stages of possession. Here are four of them:

Manifestation - Is when the entity is invited in, intentionally or unintentionally.

Infestation - Is when the entity makes itself known to you. You may have the feeling of being watched; scratching or knocking on the walls, whispers, and other paranormal activity.

Oppression - One of their favorite tactics is to weaken your will by making it difficult for you to sleep. They will also expose any weaknesses, fears, guilt or grief, and use them as a trigger.

Possession - Is when your active free will has been breached, and the entity has access to your body.

PRECOGNITION - Seeing or knowing activity received from the future using ESP.

PREMONITION - A psychic awareness of future events, often with a negative outcome.

PSI - A general term for para psychological phenomenon.

PSYCHIC - A person who is sensitive beyond the normal means. May be able to see, and hear things that are not available to most people.

PSYCHOKINESIS - To move something with the powers of one's mind. Usually associated with poltergeist activity.

RECIPROCAL APPARITION - A rare type of ghost sighting when both the spirit, and the human witness see, and respond to one another.

RESIDUAL HAUNTING - A repeated haunting in which no intelligent entity or spirit is directly involved. This is the playback of a past event, trapped in a continuous loop. It is often associated with past events involving great trauma or tragedy.

RETROCOGNITION - Seeing or knowing activity from the past using ESP.

SEANCE - A meeting of individuals in order to contact the spirit of a deceased loved one or other person (usually consisting of a medium, assistants, loved ones of the departed, or other interested individuals).

SENSITIVE - A person who professes an ability to perceive information through extrasensory perception (ESP).

SHADOW PERSON - A dark fleeting entity seen out of the corner of the eye.

SMUDGING – A cleansing technique with Native American roots, where a dried herb bundle or sweet grass is burned for purification.

SOUL - A soul, in certain spiritual, philosophical, and psychological traditions, is the corporeal essence of a person of living thing or object.

SPECTER - Another term for a ghost.

SPIRIT - The actual consciousness or soul of an individual that has passed on, and continues to be observed in an area. They have actually gone through the light but are able to come and go between the physical world, and the afterlife.

SPIRIT ATTACHMENT - When a spirit attaches itself to another person or inanimate object.

SPIRIT REALM - World inhabited by spirits.

SPIRITUALISM - The belief system that the dead are able to communicate with the living, most often through an intermediary or medium.

SUBJECTIVE APPARITION - Hallucination of apparitions or other phenomenon that are created by our own minds.

SUCCUBUS - A female demon appearing in dreams, who takes the form of a human woman in order to seduce men, usually through sexual intercourse.

SUPERNATURAL - Events or happenings that take place in violation of the laws of nature, usually associated with ghosts, and hauntings.

TELEKINESIS - The ability to control one's physical environment without using physical manipulation or force (also known as psycho kinesis, TK, or PK). Usually associated with poltergeist activity.

TELEPATHY - The process by which the mind can communicate directly with another without using normal, physical interaction or ordinary sensory perception.

TELEPORTATION - A method of transportation in which matter or information is dematerialized, usually instantaneously, at one point, and recreated at another.

VORTEX - The center of paranormal activity thought to be an actual portal to the spirit realm.

WANDERING SPIRIT - A spirit who wanders, and briefly stays at a location until their curiosity abates.

WARP - A location where the known laws of physics do not always apply, and space/time may be distorted.

WHITE NOISE - A sound, such as running water, which masks all speech sounds. Used in collection of EVPs'.

WRAITH - An apparition of a living person that appears as a portent, just before that person's death.

Appendix II

CLIENT QUESTIONNAIRE

 ## *TRI-C GHOST HUNTERS*

Client Questionnaire

Date of Interview_____Investigator_____

Location Information

Address of Investigation_____

Occupant Information

Number of Occupants at Living at Location_____

Names, Gender, Relationship and Ages of Occupants (Add Additional to Back of Sheet)

1._____
2._____
3._____
4._____
5._____
6._____

Any Pets?_____

Phone_____E-Mail_____

Mailing Address_____

_____
_____
_____
_____

Occupant Information

How long have occupants lived at location? _____

When did activity start? _____

Have any of the occupants encountered any of the following? (Check all that apply.):

☐ Voices - explain: _____
☐ Smells/Odors – explain: _____
☐ Shadows explain: _____
☐ Orbs – explain: _____
☐ Smoky Forms – explain: _____
☐ Strong Random Thoughts – explain: _____

☐ Cold or Hot Spots – explain: _____
☐ Recent Death of Loved Ones give info: _____
☐ Recent Anniversary of Loved One's Death, Birthday, Anniversary, etc. _____
☐ Rapping's or Knockings explain: _____
☐ Door(s) Opening/Closing – explain: _____
☐ Mood Changes, especially in one room – explain: _____

☐ Conversations with Spirit – explain: _____

☐ Moving/Disappearing Objects – explain: _____
☐ Electrical Disturbances – explain: _____

☐ Puberty of Family Member or Emotional Stress of Adolescents in Area – explain: _____

☐ Renovations in Location – explain: _____

☐ Problems with Appliances:

    ☐ TV
    ☐ Radio/Stereo
    ☐ Computer
    ☐ Clock/Clock Radio
    ☐ Microwave
    ☐ Other: _____

Notes

Appendix III

PARANORMAL MOVIES

The following is a list of movies dealing with the paranormal, ghosts, the supernatural, possession, demons and haunted houses, and the year they were released. The list is not all inclusive as I am sure I missed numerous movies that would fit into any one of those categories. You may also find movies listed that do not necessarily fit. If so, or if you have a movie to add just email me at gefeketik@gmail.com.

100 Feet	(2008)
11-11-11	(2011)
12/12/12	(2012)
13 Ghosts	(1960)
1408	(2007)
2001 Maniacs	(2005)
7 Nights of Darkness	(2011)
976-EVIL	(1988)
A Christmas Carol	(2004)
A Christmas Carol	(2006)
A Christmas Carol	(2009)
A Guy Named Joe	(1943)
A Haunted House 2	(2014)
A Haunted House	(2013)
A Haunting at Silver Falls	(2013)
A Haunting We Will Go	(1942)
A Nightmare on Elm Street	(1984)
A Nightmare on Elm Street 2: Freddy's Revenge	(1985)
A Nightmare on Elm Street 3: Dream Warriors	(1987)
A Nightmare on Elm Street 4: The Dream Master	(1988)
A Nightmare on Elm Street 5: The Dream Child	(1989)
A Place of One's Own	(1945)

Abandoned (The)	(2015)
Abby	(1974)
Absentia	(2011)
Alleluia! The Devil's Carnival	(2016)
Always	(1989)
Amityville 3-D	(1983)
Amityville 4: The Evil Escapes	(1989)
Amityville Asylum (The)	(2013)
Amityville Curse (The)	(1990)
Amityville Death House	(2015)
Amityville Dollhouse	(1996)
Amityville Haunting (The)	(2011)
Amityville Horror	(1979)
Amityville Horror	(2005)
Amityville II: The Possession	(1982)
Amityville Legacy (The)	(2016)
Amityville Playhouse (The)	(2015)
Amityville Terror (The)	(2016)
Amityville: A New Generation	(1993)
Amityville: It's About Time	(1992)
Amityville: No Escape	(2016)
Amityville: The Awakening	(2017)
Amityville: The Reawakening	(2016)
Amityville: Vanishing Point	(2016)
An American Haunting	(2005)
Anguish	(2015)
Annabelle	(2014)
Annabelle: Creation	(2017)
Apartment 1303	(2007)
Apparition (The)	(2012)
Appearing (The)	(2014)
Asylum	(2008)
At the Devil's Door	(2014)
Atoning (The)	(2017)
Audrey Rose	(1977)
Autopsy of Jane Doe (The)	(2016)

Ava's Possessions	(2015)
Avenged	(2013)
Babadook (The)	(2014)
Back from the Dead	(1957)
Ballerina (The)	(2017)
Bedeviled	(2016)
Beetlejuice	(1988)
Believe	(1999)
Bell Witch Haunting (The)	(2013)
Bell Witch: The Movie	(2007)
Below	(2002)
Beyond Evil	(1980)
Beyond the Door	(1974)
Beyond Tomorrow	(1940)
Black Devil Doll from Hell	(1984)
Blackbeard's Ghost	(1968)
Blackcoat's Daughter (The)	(2015)
Blair Witch	(2016)
Blair Witch Project (The)	(1999)
Bless the Child	(2000)
Blithe Spirit	(1945)
Blood Night: The Legend of Mary Hatchet	(2009)
Bloody Mary	(2006)
Bones	(2001)
Boo	(2005)
Boogeyman	(2005)
Boogeyman 3	(2008)
Boogeyman (The)	(1980)
Book of Blood	(2009)
Book of Life (The)	(2014)
Burnt Offerings	(1976)
Bye Bye Man (The)	(2017)
Calling (The)	(2000)
Cameron's Closet	(1988)
Canterville Ghost (The)	(1944)
Canterville Ghost (The)	(1985)

Canterville Ghost (The)	(1986)
Canterville Ghost (The)	(1996)
Carnival of Souls	(1962)
Carrie	(1976)
Carrie	(2002)
Carrie	(2013)
Casper	(1995)
Catacombs	(1988)
Changeling (The)	(1980)
Child's Play	(1988)
Chosen (The)	(2015)
Christine	(1983)
Christmas Carol: The Movie	(2001)
Closed for the Season	(2010)
Cloth (The)	(2013)
Cockeyed Miracle (The)	(1946)
Conjurer	(2008)
Conjuring (The)	(2013)
Conjuring 2: The Enfield Poltergeist	(2016)
Constantine	(2005)
Convent (The)	(2000)
Convergence	(2015)
Corpse Bride	(2005)
Covenant (The)	(2006)
Crimson Peak	(2015)
Crucifixion (The)	(2017)
Culling (The)	(2015)
Curse of the Crying Woman (The)	(1961)
Damien: Omen II	(1978)
Damned (The)	(2013)
Dark Angel: The Ascent	(1994)
Dark House	(2009)
Dark Remains	(2005)
Dark Summer	(2015)
Dark Tapes (The)	(2016)
Dark Water	(2002)

Dark Water	(2005)
Darkness	(2002)
Darkness Falls	(2003)
Darkness	(2002)
Darkness (The)	(2016)
Dead Awake	(2016)
Dead Birds	(2004)
Dead of Night	(1945)
Dead Silence	(2007)
Dead Zone (The)	(1983)
Death Becomes Her	(1992)
Death Bed: The Bed That Eats	(1977)
Death of a Ghost Hunter	(2007)
Deliver Us from Evil	(2014)
Demonic	(2015)
Demons	(2017)
Desecration	(1999)
Detention	(2010)
Devil	(2010)
Devil Inside (The)	(2012)
Devil's Advocate (The)	(1997)
Devil's Backbone (The)	(2001)
Devil's Candy (The)	(2015)
Devil's Due	(2014)
Devil's Highway	(2005)
Devil's Rain (The)	(1975)
Devil's Whisper	(2017)
Don't be Afraid of the Dark	(1973)
Don't be Afraid of the Dark	(2010)
Don't Take It to Heart	(1944)
Doppelganger	(1993)
Down a Dark Hall	(2018)
Drag Me to Hell	(2009)
Echo (The)	(2008)
Encounter with the Unknown	(1973)
End of Days	(1999)

Entity (The)	(1981)
Evil Dead	(2013)
Evil Dead (The)	(1981)
Evil Within (The)	(2017)
Evil (The)	(1978)
Evilspeak	(1981)
Exeter	(2015)
Exorcism of Emily Rose (The)	(2005)
Exorcist (The)	(1973)
Exorcist II: The Heretic	(1977)
Exorcist III, The	(1990)
Exorcist: The Beginning	(2004)
Eye (The)	(2002)
Eye (The)	(2008)
Eye 10 (The)	(2005)
Eye 2 (The)	(2004)
Eyes of Fire	(1984)
Fading of the Cries	(2010)
FeardotCom	(2002)
Fever Night aka Band of Satanic Outsiders	(2009)
Fiend	(1980)
Final Project (The)	(2015)
Finders Keepers	(2014)
Fingerprints	(2006)
Flatliners	(1990)
Flatliners	(2017)
Flesh for the Beast	(2003)
Flight 7500	(2014)
Fog (The)	(1980)
Fog (The)	(2005)
Forest (The)	(2016)
Found Footage 3D	(2016)
Freddy vs. Jason	(2003)
Freddy's Dead: The Final Nightmare	(1994)
Frighteners (The)	(1996)
From Within	(2008)

Gallows (The)	(2015)
Gallows 2 (The)	(2018)
Ghost	(1990)
Ghost and Mrs. Muir (The)	(1947)
Ghost Breakers (The)	(1940)
Ghost Chasers	(1951)
Ghost Dad	(1990)
Ghost Dad	(1990)
Ghost Goes West (The)	(1936)
Ghost in the Machine	(1993)
Ghost of Berkeley Square (The)	(1947)
Ghost of Flight 401 (The)	(1978)
Ghost of Greville Lodge (The)	(2000)
Ghost Rider	(2006)
Ghost Ship	(2002)
Ghost Story	(1981)
Ghost Story	(1981)
Ghost Talks (The)	(1949)
Ghost Town	(2008)
Ghost Town	(2008)
Ghost Walks (The)	(1934)
Ghostbusters	(1984)
Ghostbusters II	(1989)
Ghosts of Edendale (The)	(2004)
Ghosts of Mars	(2001)
Gift (The)	(2000)
Gildersleeve's Ghost	(1944)
Gothika	(2003)
Gourmet (The)	(1984)
Grave Encounters	(2011)
Grave Secrets: The Legacy of Hilltop Drive	(1992)
Gravedancers (The)	(2006)
Grudge (The)	(2004)
Grudge 2 (The)	(2006)
Grudge 3 (The)	(2009)
Grudge (The)	(2019)

Halloween Tree (The)	(1993)
Haunted	(1995)
Haunted Castle (The)	(1921)
Haunted House (The)	(1921)
Haunted House	(2004)
Haunted Lighthouse	(2003)
Haunted Mansion (The)	(2003)
Haunted Sea (The)	(1997)
Haunting (The)	(1963)
Haunting (The)	(1999)
Haunting in Connecticut (The)	(2009)
Haunting in Connecticut (The): Ghosts of Georgia	(2013)
Haunting of Cell Block 11	(2014)
Haunting of Helena (The)	(2012)
Haunting of Hell House, (The)	(1999)
Haunting of Molly Hartley (The)	(2008)
Haunting of Whaley House (The)	(2012)
Haunting Sarah	(2005)
Heart and Souls	(1993)
Hereditary	(2018)
High Spirits	(1988)
Hold That Ghost	(1941)
House	(1986)
House II: The Second Story	(1987)
House IV	(1992)
House on Haunted Hill	(1959)
House on Haunted Hill	(1999)
House Where Evil Dwells (The)	(1982)
Husk	(2011)
Incarnate	(2016)
Incubus	(1966)
Inkubus	(2011)
Innocents (The)	(1961)
Insidious	(2011)
Insidious 2	(2013)
Insidious: Chapter 3	(2015)

Insidious: The Last Key	(2018)
Into the Dark	(2012)
It	(1990)
It – Chapter Two	(2019)
It	(2017)
It Follows	(2014)
Jennifer's Body	(2009)
Jessabelle	(2014)
Jingles the Clown	(2009)
Jolly Roger: Massacre at Cutter's Cove	(2005)
Ju-on: The Grudge	(2003)
Just Like Heaven	(2005)
Kairo	(2001)
Keeping Hours (The)	(2017)
Kwaidan	(1964)
Lady in White	(1988)
Lani Loa - The Passage	(1998)
Last Exorcism (The)	(2010)
Lazarus Effect (The)	(2015)
Legend of Hell House	(1973)
Legion	(2010)
Let's Scare Jessica to Death	(1971)
Lights Out	(2016)
Lonesome Ghost	(1937)
Look What's Happened to Rosemary's Baby	(1976)
Lovely Bones (The)	(2009)
Maid (The)	(2005)
Mama	(2013)
Man in the Maze (The)	(2011)
Maxie	(1985)
Mercy	(2014)
Messengers (The)	(2007)
Mirror, Mirror	(1990)
Mirror, Mirror II: Raven Dance	(1994)
Mirrors	(2008)
Mirrors 2	(2010)

Mostly Ghostly: Have You Met My Ghoulfriend?	(2014)
Mostly Ghostly: Who Let the Ghosts Out?	(2008)
Muck	(2015)
Nang Nak	(1999)
Night of Dark Shadows	(1971)
Nightmare Before Christmas (The)	(1993)
Nomads	(1986)
Nothing Left to Fear	(2013)
Nun (The)	(2018)
Nurse (The)	(2017)
Oculus	(2013)
Old Dark House (The)	(1963)
Old Mother Riley's Ghosts	(1941)
Omen (The)	(1976)
Omen III: The Final Conflict	(1981)
Omen (The)	(2006)
One Dark Night	(1983)
One Missed Call	(2008)
Orphanage (The)	(2007)
Other (The)	(1972)
Other Side of the Tracks (The)	(2008)
Others (The)	(2001)
Ouija	(2014)
Ouija House	(2018)
Ouija: Origin of Evil	(2016)
Over Her Dead Body	(2008)
Pandora and the Flying Dutchman	(1951)
Paranormal Activity	(2007)
Paranormal Activity 2	(2010)
Paranormal Activity 3	(2011)
Paranormal Activity 4	(2012)
Paranormal Activity: The Ghost Dimension	(2015)
Paranormal Activity: The Marked Ones	(2014)
ParaNorman	(2012)
Pernicious	(2014)
Pet Sematary	(1989)

Pet Sematary	(2019)
Pet Sematary Two	(1992)
Poltergeist	(1982)
Poltergeist	(2015)
Poltergeist II	(1986)
Poltergeist III	(1988)
Poltergeist	(2015)
Portrait of Jennie	(1948)
Power (The)	(1984)
Practical Magic	(1998)
Presence (The)	(2010)
Prince of Darkness	(1987)
Pulse	(2006)
R.I.P.D.	(2013)
Rage: Carrie 2 (The)	(1999)
Return to House on Haunted Hill	(2007)
Riding the Bullet	(2004)
Ring (The)	(2002)
Ring Two (The)	(2005)
Rings	(2017)
Ringu	(1998)
Ringu 2	(1999)
Rinne	(2006)
Rosemary's Baby	(1968)
Route 666	(2001)
Ruby	(1977)
Saint Ange	(2004)
Satan War	(1979)
Scared Stiff	(1953)
Scary Movie 2	(2001)
Scary Movie 3	(2003)
Scary Movie 4	(2006)
Scary Movie 5	(2013)
Schalcken the Painter	(1979)
School Spirit	(1985)
Scooby Doo	(2002)

Scooby Doo 2: Monsters Unleashed	(2004)
Screaming Skull (The)	(1958)
Scrooge	(1913)
Scrooge	(1935)
Scrooge	(1951)
Scrooged	(1988)
Sentinel (The)	(1977)
Session 9	(2001)
Shadow of Chikara (The)	(1977)
Shining (The)	(1980)
Shock	(2004)
Shutter	(2008)
Silent Hill	(2006)
Silent Tongue	(1993)
Sinister	(2012)
Sinister 2	(2015)
Sixth Man (The)	(1997)
Sixth Sense (The)	(1999)
Skeleton Key, (The)	(2005)
Slaughterhouse Rock	(1988)
Sleeping Soul (The)	(2012)
Sleepy Hollow	(1999)
Slender Man	(2018)
Smiling Ghost (The)	(1941)
Solstice	(2008)
Someone Behind You	(2007)
Soul Survivors	(2001)
Spell (The)	(1977)
Spirit in the Woods	(2014)
Spirit is Willing (The)	(1967)
Spook Busters	(1946)
St. Francisville Experiment (The)	(2000)
Stay Alive	(2006)
Stephanie	(2017)
Stigmata	(1999)
Stir of Echoes	(1999)

Stir of Echoes 2: The Homecoming	(2007)
Street Trash	(1999)
Susie Q	(1996)
Suspiria	(1977)
Suspiria	(2018)
Sx_Tape	(2013)
Tales of Terror	(1962)
Terror (The)	(1963)
Terror in the Haunted House	(1958)
Thirteen Ghosts	(2001)
Time of Their Lives (The)	(1946)
Topper	(1937)
Topper Returns	(1941)
Topper Takes a Trip	(1938)
Tormented	(2009)
Tormented	(1960)
Totem	(2017)
Tower of Terror	(1997)
Toybox (The)	(2018)
Trick or Treat	(1986)
Truly, Madly, Deeply	(1990)
Truth or Dare	(2017)
Two Thousand Maniacs!	(1964)
Unfriended	(2014)
Uninvited (The)	(1944)
Uninvited (The)	(2008)
Uninvited (The)	(2009)
Urban Legends: Bloody Mary	(2005)
Vatican Tapes (The)	(2015)
Venom	(2005)
Watcher in the Woods (The)	(1980)
We Are Still Here	(2015)
Wes Craven's New Nightmare	(1994)
What Lies Beneath	(2000)
Where Got Ghost?	(2009)
White Noise	(2005)

Appendix IV

<u>PHOTO CREDITS</u>

Front Cover - Designed by Greg Feketik. Photograph obtained through iStock by Getty Images. www.istockphoto.com. Credit: Lisa Valder.

Photo 1 - Photograph by Greg Feketik, used with permission of the Summit Metro Park system, www.summitmetroparks.org

Photo 2 - Photograph by Allison Feketik, used with permission of the Summit Metro Park system, www.summitmetroparks.org.

Photo 3 - Photograph by Allison Feketik, used with permission of the Summit Metro Park system, www.summitmetroparks.org.

Photo 4 - Photograph by Allison Feketik, used with permission of the Summit Metro Park system, www.summitmetroparks.org.

Photo 5 – Photograph by Allison Feketik, used with permission of the Summit Metro Park system, www.summitmetroparks.org.

Photo 6 - Photograph by Allison Feketik, used with permission of the Summit Metro Park system, www.summitmetroparks.org.

Photo 7 - Photograph by Allison Feketik, used with permission of the Summit Metro Park system, www.summitmetroparks.org.

Photo 8 - Photograph by Greg Feketik. Used with permission of the Lemp Mansion, www.lempmansion.com.

Photo 9 - Photograph by Greg Feketik. Used with permission of the Lemp Mansion, www.lempmansion.com.

Photo 10 - Photograph by Greg Feketik. Used with permission of the Lemp Mansion, www.lempmansion.com.

Photo 11 - Photograph by Greg Feketik. Used with permission of Sharyn Luedke, the McPike Mansion, www.mcpikemansion.com.

Photo 12 - Photograph by Greg Feketik. Used with permission of Sharyn Luedke, the McPike Mansion, www.mcpikemansion.com.

Photo 13 - Photograph by Greg Feketik. Used with permission of Sharyn Luedke, the McPike Mansion, www.mcpikemansion.com.

Photo 14 - Photograph courtesy of the Rubel Hotel, www.ruebelhotel.com.

Photo 15 - Photograph courtesy of the Rubel Hotel, www.ruebelhotel.com.

Photo 16 - Photograph by Greg Feketik. Used with permission of the Ruebel Hotel, www.ruebelhotel.com.

Photo 17 - Photograph courtesy of the Rubel Hotel, www.ruebelhotel.com.

Photo 18 - Photograph by Arlene Feketik.

Photo 19 - Photograph by Greg Feketik.

Photo 20 - Photograph by Greg Feketik.

Photo 21 - Photograph by Greg Feketik.

Photo 22 – Photograph by Greg Feketik.

Photo 23 – Photograph by Greg Feketik.

Photo 24 – Photograph by Greg Feketik. Used with permission of Historic Royal Palaces, www.images.hrp.org.uk//en/page/show_home_page.html

Photo 25 – Photograph by Greg Feketik, used with permission of Janice McBride McCreadie.

Photo 26 – Photograph by Greg Feketik. Used with permission of the Rosslyn Chapel Trust, www.rosslynchapel.com.

Photo 27 – Photograph courtesy of the Rosslyn Chapel Trust, www.rosslynchapel.com.

Photo 28 - Photograph by Greg Feketik. Used with permission of Edinburgh City Council, Parks, Green Space and Cemeteries Service, www.edinburgh.gov.uk.

Photo 29 - Photograph by Greg Feketik. Used with permission of Edinburgh City Council, Parks, Green Space and Cemeteries Service, www.edinburgh.gov.uk.

Photo 30 - Photograph by Greg Feketik. Used with permission of Edinburgh City Council, Parks, Green Space and Cemeteries Service, www.edinburgh.gov.uk.

Photo 31 - Photograph by Greg Feketik. Used with permission of Edinburgh City Council, Parks, Green Space and Cemeteries Service, www.edinburgh.gov.uk.

Photo 32 - Photograph by Greg Feketik. Used with permission of Day of the Dead Tours, www.cityofthedeadtours.com.

Photo 33 - Photograph by Greg Feketik. Used with permission of Day of the Dead Tours, www.cityofthedeadtours.com.

Photo 34 - Photograph by Greg Feketik. Used with permission of Day of the Dead Tours, www.cityofthedeadtours.com.

Photo 35 – Photograph by Greg Feketik. Used with permission of Dalhousie Castle, www.dalhousiecastle.com.

Photo 36 – Photograph by Greg Feketik. Used with permission of Dalhousie Castle, www.dalhousiecastle.com.

Photo 37 – Photograph by Kathy Feketik. Used with permission of Dalhousie Castle, www.dalhousiecastle.com.

Photo 38 – Photograph by Kathy Feketik. Used with permission of Dalhousie Castle, www.dalhousiecastle.com.

Photo 39 – Photograph by Kathy Feketik. Used with permission of Dalhousie Castle, www.dalhousiecastle.com.

Photo 40 – Photograph taken by a friend.

Photo 41 – Photograph by Greg Feketik. Used with permission of the Myrtles Plantation, www.myrtlesplantation.com.

Photo 42 – Photograph by Shelley Grant. Used with permission of the Myrtles Plantation, www.myrtlesplantation.com.

Photo 43 – Photograph by Greg Feketik. Used with permission of the Myrtles Plantation, www.myrtlesplantation.com.

Photo 44 – Photograph by Greg Feketik. Used with permission of the Myrtles Plantation, www.myrtlesplantation.com.

Photo 45 – Photograph by Greg Feketik. Used with permission of the Myrtles Plantation, www.myrtlesplantation.com.

Photo 46 – Photograph by Greg Feketik. Used with permission of the Myrtles Plantation, www.myrtlesplantation.com.

Photo 47 – Photograph by Greg Feketik. Used with permission of the Myrtles Plantation, www.myrtlesplantation.com.

Photo 48 - Photograph by Greg Feketik. Used with permission of the Roads Hotel, www.rhoadshotel.com.

Photo 49 - Photograph by Greg Feketik. Used with permission of the Roads Hotel, www.rhoadshotel.com.

Photo 50 - Photograph by Greg Feketik. Used with permission of the Roads Hotel, www.rhoadshotel.com.

Photo 51 - Photograph by Greg Feketik. Used with permission of the Roads Hotel, www.rhoadshotel.com.

Photo 52 - Photograph by Greg Feketik. Used with permission of the Roads Hotel, www.rhoadshotel.com.

Photo 53 - Photograph by Greg Feketik. Used with permission of the Roads Hotel, www.rhoadshotel.com.

Photo 54 - Photograph by Greg Feketik. Used with permission of the Roads Hotel, www.rhoadshotel.com.

Photo 55 - Photograph by Greg Feketik. Used with permission of St. Joseph Hospital, South Shore Community Development Corporation.

Photo 56 - Photograph by Greg Feketik. Used with permission of St. Joseph Hospital, South Shore Community Development Corporation.

Photo 57 - Photograph by Greg Feketik. Used with permission of St. Joseph Hospital, South Shore Community Development Corporation.

Appendix V

<u>REFERENCES/END NOTES</u>

[1] www.theharrispoll.com/new-york-n-y-december-16-2013-a-new-harris-poll-finds-that-while-a-strong-majority-74-of-u-s-adults-do-believe-in-god-this-belief-is-in-decline-when-compared-to-previous-years-as-just-over/

[2] www.biblestudytools.com/passage/?q=jesaja+14:12-15;+hesekiel+28:12-19

[3] www.imdb.com/title/tt0089175/?ref_=fn_al_tt_1

[4] www.biblegateway.com/passage/?search=Genesis+1%3A27&version=NIV

[5] www.thoughtco.com/counting-habitable-planets-3072596

[6] www.en.wikipedia.org/wiki/Chariots_of_the_Gods%3F

[7] www.en.wikipedia.org/wiki/Gigantopithecus

[8] www.en.wikipedia.org/wiki/Coelacanth

[9] www.medium.com/@metro_parks/history-and-mystery-of-the-indian-signal-tree-fc6866d7b2d3

[10] www.prairieghosts.com/lemp.html

[11] www.en.wikipedia.org/wiki/Lemp_Mansion

[12] www.en.wikipedia.org/wiki/Lemp_Mansion

[13] www.en.wikipedia.org/wiki/Lemp_Mansion

[14] www.en.wikipedia.org/wiki/Lemp_Mansion

[15] www.en.wikipedia.org/wiki/Lemp_Mansion

[16] www.en.wikipedia.org/wiki/Lemp_Mansion

[17] www.gothichorrorstories.com/true-ghost-stories/the-best-haunted-hotels-and-inns-a-house-built-on-beer-brought-down-by-suicides-and-debauchery-makes-for-a-great-ghoulish-destination/

[18] www.altonhauntings.com

[19] www.en.wikipedia.org/wiki/Alton,_Illinois

[20]www.en.wikipedia.org/wiki/Robert_Wadlow

[21] www.altonweb.com/history/civilwar/confed/

[22] www.mcpikemansion.com/history.html

[23] www.en.wikipedia.org/wiki/Grafton,_Illinois

[24] www.ruebelhotel.com/our-history

[25] www.mysteriousheartland.com/2011/07/18/top-10-most-haunted-hotels-in-illinois/

[26] www.onlyinyourstate.com/illinois/creepy-hotel-il/

[27] www.en.wikipedia.org/wiki/North_Olmsted,_Ohio

[28] www.wellnessmama.com/129645/emf-exposure/

[29] www.beinglight.com/products/emfchart.htm

[30] www.en.wikipedia.org/wiki/Coccinellidae

[31] www.infinitespider.com/ladybugs-bite-surprising-answer/

[32] www.firsttoknow.com/why-children-can-see-ghosts/

[33] www.destinationamerica.com/thehauntist/when-kids-really-do-see-dead-people/

[34] www.firsttoknow.com/why-children-can-see-ghosts/

[35] www.en.wikipedia.org/wiki/Tower_of_London

[36] www.en.wikipedia.org/wiki/Tower_Green

[37] www.historic-uk.com/HistoryUK/HistoryofEngland/Torture-in-the-Tower-of-London/

[38] www.hauntedencounters.wordpress.com/2015/06/07/the-headless-ghost-of-anne-boleyn/

[39] www.mysticfiles.com/the-amazing-and-haunted-tower-of-london/

[40] www.en.wikipedia.org/wiki/Henry_Walpole

[41] www.thelondonbridgeexperience.com/

[42] www.en.wikipedia.org/wiki/Royal_Mile

[43] www.en.wikipedia.org/wiki/Edinburgh_Castle

[44] www.visitscotland.com/blog/scotland/haunted-sites/

[45] www.scotsman.com/news/edinburgh-is-the-place-to-be-for-ghostly-goings-on-1-2607073

[46] www.en.wikipedia.org/wiki/Penicuik_House

[47] www.penicuikhouse.co.uk/about-us/the-trust/our-vision/

[48] www.en.wikipedia.org/wiki/Rosslyn_Chapel

[49] www.hauntedrooms.co.uk/most-haunted-places-in-scotland-scary-locations

[50] www.europeupclose.com/article/the-many-mysteries-of-rosslyn-chapel/

[51] www.en.wikipedia.org/wiki/Greyfriars_Kirkyard

[52] www.covenanter.org.uk/greyfriars_prison.html

[53] www.historicmysteries.com/mackenzie-poltergeist-greyfriars/

[54] www.britannica.com/event/National-Covenant

[55] www.en.wikipedia.org/wiki/George_Mackenzie_of_Rosehaugh

[56] www.en.wikipedia.org/wiki/Battle_of_Bothwell_Bridge

[57] www.en.wikipedia.org/wiki/Edinburgh_Vaults

[58] www.en.wikipedia.org/wiki/Dalhousie_Castle

[59] www.dalhousiecastle.co.uk/

[60] www.ruraltravelguide.co.uk/rtghome/2017/10/18/is-this-scotlands-most-haunted-castle

[61] www.scotsman.com/lifestyle/culture/books/looking-for-ghosts-try-the-usual-haunts-1-1021646

[62] www.everythingghost.co.uk/forum/viewtopic.php?f=29&t=643

[63] www.en.wikipedia.org/wiki/Castle_Stuart

[64] www.didyouknowfacts.com/facts/did-you-kno-medieval-castle-stairs-were-often/

[65] www.hauntedspotslibrary.wordpress.com/2017/04/08/castle-stuart-strange-connections-and-hauntings-that-kill/

[66] www.en.wikipedia.org/wiki/Loch_Ness

[67] www.en.wikipedia.org/wiki/Loch_Ness_Monster

[68] www.en.wikipedia.org/wiki/List_of_Unsolved_Mysteries_episodes

[69] www.imdb.com/title/tt0218625/

[70] www.amazon.com/Myrtles-Plantation-Story-Americas-Haunted/dp/0446614157

[71] www.en.wikipedia.org/wiki/Myrtles_Plantation

[72] www.en.wikipedia.org/wiki/Whiskey_Rebellion

[73] www.myrtlesplantation.com/

[74] www.en.wikipedia.org/wiki/Myrtles_Plantation

[75] www.en.wikipedia.org/wiki/Legends_of_Myrtles_Plantation

[76] www.en.wikipedia.org/wiki/Legends_of_Myrtles_Plantation

[77] www.atlantaindiana.com/community/history

[78] www.en.wikipedia.org/wiki/Atlanta,_Indiana

[79] Emails from Jodi, Roads Hotel, June 1, 2016

[80] www.ss-times.com/haunts-jaunts-roads-hotel/

[81] www.awesomestories.com/asset/view/John-Dillinger-List-of-His-Bank-Robberies//1

[82] www.lorainpubliclibrary.org/research/local-research/local-history-resources/history-of-lorain-ohio--chronology

[83] www.stfrancistiffin.org/home/history/

[84] www.en.wikipedia.org/wiki/Lorain,_Ohio

[85] www.en.wikipedia.org/wiki/Lorain,_Ohio

[86] www.ohiohistorycentral.org/w/1924_Lorain_Tornado

[87] www.ancientstandard.com/2007/10/31/an-ancient-roman-ghost-story-ca-61-115-ad/

[88] www.merriam-webster.com/dictionary/scientific%20method

[89] www.amazon.com/Art-Science-Paranormal-Investigation/dp/1466265884

[90] www.science.howstuffworks.com/10-inventions-thomas-edison10.htm

[91] www.eidolonparanormal.blogspot.com/2013/05/paranormal-investigators-past-present_19.html

[92] www.vtf.de/websites/www.paravoice.dk/jurgenson's%20first%20book.htm

OTHER BOOKS

Insights into the Unknown: A Ghost Hunter's Journey

A collections of real life paranormal experiences by author Greg Feketik.

Published September 17, 2015 by CreateSpace Independent Publisher Platform - 174 pages.

ISBN: 9781517300326

Amazing Paranormal Encounters Vol. 3

A collection of real experiences by notable paranormal personalities, by various authors, including Greg Feketik.

Published April 21, 2016 by CreateSpace Independent Publisher Platform – 164 pages.

ISBN: 9781537218182

Amazing Paranormal Encounters Vol. 4

A collection of real experiences by notable paranormal personalities, by various authors, including Greg Feketik.

Published April 30, 2017 by CreateSpace Independent Publisher Platform – 158 pages.

ISBN: 978155461620X

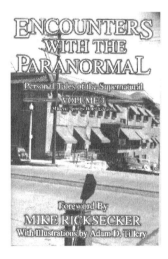

Encounters with the Paranormal Vol. 3 – Personal Tales of the Supernatural

A collection of real paranormal encounters by various authors, including Greg Feketik.

Published October 11, 2017 by Haunted Road Media, LLC – 146 pages.

ISBN: 9780998164939

All books available on Amazon.

Made in the USA
Columbia, SC
20 March 2019